IF YOU
LIVED HERE
YOU'D BE
HOME BY NOW

IF YOU
LIVED HERE
YOU'D BE
HOME BY NOW

Why We Traded the
Commuting Life for a Little
House on the Prairie

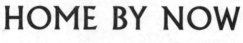

CHRISTOPHER INGRAHAM

HARPER

An Imprint of HarperCollinsPublishers

HarperCollins books may be purchased for educational, business, or sales promotional use. For information, please email the Special Markets Department at SPsales@harpercollins.com.

FIRST EDITION

Portions of chapter 1 have previously appeared in a different form in the *Washington Post* story "I Called This Place 'America's Worst Place to Live.' Then I Went There."

Portions of chapter 5 have previously appeared in a different form in the *Washington Post* story "I Ordered a Box of Crickets from the Internet and It Went About as Well as You'd Expect."

Portions of chapter 8 have previously appeared in a different form in the *Washington Post* story "Why These Rural, White, Gun-Owning Guys Didn't Vote for Trump."

Portions of chapter 3, chapter 5, and the epilogue have previously appeared in a different form in the *Washington Post* story "What Life Is Really Like in 'America's Worst Place to Live.'"

Illustration by Vector Bang/Shutterstock, Inc.

Library of Congress Cataloging-in-Publication Data has been applied for.

ISBN 978-0-06-286147-4

19 20 21 22 23   LSC   10 9 8 7 6 5 4 3 2

To Briana

IF YOU
LIVED HERE
YOU'D BE
HOME BY NOW

PROLOGUE

It's cold. Not *really* cold, mind you—none of that minus-twenty-or-forty business we'll get later in the season. But the mercury's somewhere just south of zero, the winds are whipping like mad up and down the frozen river, and the twins are getting bored.

"Daddy, when can we go?" Charles asks. A certain falling inflection on the "Dad-dy" suggests he's about five minutes away from losing it completely, melting down right here on the snow. He's in his jacket, snow pants, heavy boots, mittens, neck warmer drawn up above his nose, one-size-fits-all Northern Grain hat drooping over his five-year-old head, just the way he likes it. But we've been out here too long, cold's creeping in between the layers, wind's starting to bite.

"Just a few minutes, kiddo, we're next," I tell him. I gesture over to the small playground where his twin, Jack, is gleefully whizzing down a metal slide, landing with a hard thud on the ice every single time but not minding it at all. "Why don't you go play with your brother for a few more minutes?"

"I don't want to," he says, same inflection. Despite being twins, Jack and Charles are about as different as two brothers can be. Among many other things, Jack doesn't mind the cold at all; he'll run around outside for hours until he's soaked through from the snow on the outside of his jacket and the sweat within, big clouds of hot, happy exhaled kid breath following him wherever he goes. He's a furnace. Charles, meanwhile, is hypersensitive to the cold. He's taken to insisting on having his snow pants on for even the shortest excursion outdoors, even if it's just a quick hop from the heated house to the heated car and back. He hates the feel of cold pants on his legs.

"Well then, go over there with Mom and William," I say. My wife's helping the one-year-old, our Minnesota baby, chuck fifteen-pound frozen turkeys at an assortment of short PVC pipes standing on their ends. "Turkey bowling," they call it up here. Yet another way the natives stare down the relentless winters with whimsy and good cheer. William's mostly given up on trying to manhandle the frozen birds and is basically just flinging himself down the ice alley toward the pipes. His overstuffed winter gear gives him roughly the same proportions as a bowling ball, so it's not a bad idea.

"I don't *wan*na," Charles says. He's about to go code red and I've exhausted all my other options so it's time to go nuclear: I push him down into the snow.

He's too shocked to say anything at first but I can see the rage and the laughter duking it out across his face. "*Dad*dy," he says, trying to get back up, but I knock him down again. Got 'em—he's laughing now. "DADD—" but I give him another shove before he can get it out and he's rolling around in the snow giggling. Jack hears the commotion, comes tearing over to where we are, and jumps on my back. It's on.

The three of us tumble through the snow, down the slight slope to where the deep stuff is by the river shore, among the frozen cattails still standing from the fall. I briefly wonder if one of us is going to break through some thin ice to a layer of mud or worse below but I realize that's stupid—the temperature hasn't been above freezing in months, it's barely even been above zero. The river's been frozen solid for a month at least, probably longer than that.

Soon Briana drops William on the pile and then we're all there, tumbling around in the frigid snow, the kids whooping and hollering and not even caring when one of them lands face-first in it. Suddenly Jack sits bolt upright.

"Do you hear it?" he says. We all stop and sit still. The sounds of distant baying and yipping grow louder and suddenly there they are—a team of eight lean, muscular dogs hitched to a pair of canvas sleds. It's finally our turn to run the river.

Back in the summer of 2015 I had no idea that I'd just stumbled across the dataset that would change my life, uproot me and my family from our cozy but constrained suburban D.C. life, and plop us down 1,400 miles away at the edge of the vast, open prairie. A place where it snows eight months out of the year, where winter starts in October and doesn't end until May. A place where taking the kids out on a weekend dogsledding excursion is just one of those things people do.

The dataset in question was an obscure late-1990s project of the U.S. Department of Agriculture, intended to quantify every single county in America on the physical characteristics that "enhance the location as a place to live." It assigned a score to counties based on physical characteristics—hills, valleys, bodies of water, nice weather—that most people would agree make a place pleasant to live in.

As a data reporter for the *Washington Post,* I thought I'd seen it all: numbers that explain everything from the economy to waffles to the zombie apocalypse. But here was something different—natural beauty, quantified. And with impeccable federal credentials.

Even better, the project ranked the counties according to where they fell on the scale. Which of America's more than three thousand counties are the "ugliest," according to the federal government? And which the most scenic? And where, reader, does your *own* county fall into the mix?

The story practically wrote itself, a perfect diversion for D.C.'s August recess doldrums. I mapped the numbers out, wrote a few hundred words to accompany them, slapped a headline on it all ("Every County in America, Ranked by Scenery and Climate"), and called it a day.

Like countless other pieces of data-driven ephemera I've written, I forgot about it almost as soon as my editor hit "publish" the following Monday.

Funny thing about ranking places—for every city or town or county that's at the top of some list, there has to be one all the way down at the bottom. As a country we're obsessed with superlatives—we want to raise our families in the best places, visit the most famous landmarks, climb the highest mountains, and swim the clearest, bluest seas.

But what about all those other places that don't make the cut?

This is a story about one of those forgotten places—an obscure corner of the heartland that, from the vantage point of an Excel sheet on a coastal desktop, appeared to have nothing going for it. No distinguishing features whatsoever, save a last-place finish in a county beauty pageant run by federal statisticians in the late 1990s.

Red Lake County (pop. 4,055) in northwestern Minnesota is a place so lacking in superlatives that proclaiming itself "the only landlocked county in the United States that is surrounded by just two neighboring counties" is the closest thing to a boast that you'll find on the county's website.

As it turns out, Red Lake County doesn't have any actual lakes. It doesn't have any hills. The summers are hot, and the winters are brutally cold. You crunch all those numbers together on a spreadsheet, and it may not be a surprise that the place came in dead last.

I tossed the county website's border trivia into the story along with a joke about Red Lake County being "the absolute worst place to live in America," and didn't think twice about it.

But now "the absolute worst place to live in America" is the place I and my family call home. This book is the story of how we got here, what we found when we arrived, and everything we've experienced since then. How our lives changed when we moved from one of the nation's wealthiest suburbs (median household income: $110,000) to a working-class farming community (median income: $50,000) hundreds of miles from anywhere.

It's a story about an education in the ways of small-town life. It's about the people whom I've come to call friends and neighbors, who've taught us how to fry walleye, make corn shocks, and press apple cider by hand—and who also have gently mocked our big-city "eccentricities" like goat cheese and eggplant parmesan.

But it's also bigger than that. It's a tale about two Americas—the coastal centers of power and money, like D.C., and the thousands of towns and villages in between them who feel like they've been left out of the national conversation. As the 2016 election came to a close it became clear that the gulf between those Americas is larger than it's ever been—but is it really?

It's about a journey to the other side of what social scientists call the urban-rural happiness gradient—surveys consistently show that city dwellers are the least satisfied members of society, while those who live in the countryside and small towns are the happiest.

This book is written specifically for people, like me, who are feeling increasingly stretched thin by the frenetic pace and ever-escalating cost of the big city and suburban lifestyle. People like me commuting fifteen hours a week and rarely seeing their kids because of the vast distance between where jobs are good and where housing is affordable.

People who have driven through long-forgotten rural areas on the way from one big city to another and wondered, "Who actually lives here?" People who have fantasized about throwing their big city jobs away, moving out to the middle of nowhere, and living a simpler life. People who've always wanted to raise their kids in a small town like the one they grew up in, but couldn't figure out a way to make it work.

Data from the Pew Research Center shows that more than half of Americans—54 percent—say they'd prefer to live in a small town or rural area. But more than 80 percent of us live in the cities. That's a huge disconnect—up to a third of all Americans, living in the cities but dreaming of the country.

On that icy January afternoon the mushers who were running the event helped Briana and all three kids into the front sled. The guy who was guiding us, a grizzled old former sled dog racer, climbed in the back sled.

"Wait, where am I going to go?" I asked.

"You stand on the footboards back there," he said, gesturing to the runners protruding from the sled's rear. "Hold on tight, do what I tell you, and don't fall off."

"Do you think that's wise?" I tried to ask, but by then he had given a high-pitched whistle and the dogs were off, baying with the electric excitement of animals doing the one thing in life that they were born to do.

The dogs pulled us away from shore and onto the icy expanse of the river, which meanders 193 miles from Minnesota's massive Red Lake to the Red River of the North, along the North Dakota border. Our short journey that day looped us around just a few miles of that distance, under the bridges of the town of Thief River Falls and into the open country beyond.

Once the dogs reached cruising speed they became silent, our motion along the river a frictionless glide, the only sounds the whisper of sled runners on the ice punctuated occasionally by an excited outburst from the kids in the front sled.

There used to be sled dog races all over the northern part of the country, the musher said. But not anymore. Winters were getting warmer; the sport was retreating north. Places that still got enough cold and snow to put a team of dogs out on the ice? Those places were special.

I reflected, for a moment, on the long path that had brought us here.

CHAPTER 1

What was it that stopped the train that day? "Signal problems"? Wet leaves? A body on the tracks?

The specifics didn't matter then and they sure don't matter now. All that mattered, back on that damp August morning in the summer of 2015, was that the train was running late, again. Which meant I'd be an hour, maybe two, maybe three late to work, again. Which meant I'd be staying late and not getting home until well after the kids had gone to bed. Again.

I was well into my second year writing for the *Washington Post*, a dream job by any measure. With a beat that amounted to "data, writ large" I had wide latitude in selecting topics that interested me. Bear attacks, for instance. The geography of jorts. Boats that can be parked inside other, larger boats.

My professional life, in short, was grand, except for one teeny, tiny problem. The *Washington Post* is based in Washington, D.C. My wife, Briana, and I, along with our two-year-old twins, Jack and Charles, lived just outside of Baltimore. Between our home and the *Post* newsroom lay 90 to 120 minutes of commute by car, train, subway, and foot. On a good day.

That damp August morning? Not shaping up to

be a good day. When the train finally arrived we all grumbled on. I did my best to avoid even glancing at my fellow commuters—I was never much of a people person, and chatting it up with a chipper stranger on a train, before coffee, seemed like the absolute worst way to spend that time. Some mornings I absentmindedly scrolled through my phone, searching social media for grist for the day's stories. Others I slept. Most of all, I tried not to think of how much of my life I was spending there, on the tracks, in cramped quarters surrounded by strangers.

That morning the train limped down the tracks toward D.C. much slower than usual. Eventually the train stopped, for good, about halfway to D.C. at the Bowie State University platform. There was a slight drizzle. The conductor came over the loudspeaker to inform us that the train was unable to go any further and that they had no additional information at this time.

I decided to bail, hopping off the train and calling an Uber. If I ever wanted to see my family, or my job, again, the best bet appeared to be to cut my losses, head back to Baltimore, and salvage whatever was left of the workday at home. Between the surge pricing and the distances involved, the ride cost a hundred dollars. Finally, four hours after the start of my commute, I pulled my car back into the parking space at my house. Right back where I had started.

I'm far from the only person to live like this. According to census data, roughly four million American workers, representing about 3 percent of the total sixteen-and-over workforce, have one-way commutes of ninety minutes or more. It's probably easiest for me to explain why I did: because my wife and I couldn't afford to do anything else, at least not if we were going to have our own place. According to Zillow, the median home value in Washington, D.C., is now somewhere north of half a million dollars, which was well out of the realm of affordability for Briana, then a government worker, and me.

Neither one of us came from money. I was born and raised in the village of Oneonta, an upstate New York college town of about 13,000 people situated in a kind of geographic no-man's-land between the Catskills and the Adirondacks. The region was hilly but not mountainous; populated but not populous. To the extent the

Total annual time spent commuting

Average American worker

9.3
full calendar days

Me, in 2015

31.3
full calendar days

Source: US Census Bureau

town had anything like a civic identity it was based on its adjacency to Cooperstown, home of the Baseball Hall of Fame.

My upbringing was solidly middle class for the region. My dad was a veterinarian, not a particularly glamorous career but one that provided enough money to pay the bills—or would have, had his taste for expensive status-signaling gadgets like watches, computers, and cars not put the family tens of thousands of dollars in credit card and second-mortgage debt.

My mom, a vet tech by trade, was the more pragmatic of the two. When my dad wrecked the household finances with fountain pen purchases, she did her best to restore balance by keeping the household running on generic store-brand food and thrift shop clothing. The contrast between the two provided no shortage of amusement for my high school friends, who couldn't understand why my dad was driving around town flashing his Rolex while his family ate Grand Union-brand cereal for breakfast.

My parents, in short, had a decent income but no wealth to speak of when I was growing up. They divorced my senior year in high school, a mostly amicable affair because there were no assets to fight over. After graduating from high school I made it to Cornell University in part due to my good grades, and in part due to a legacy admissions preference stemming from my dad having gone there. I ended up taking on thousands of dollars in student loan debt by the time I graduated— bills I'm still paying off today, nearly twenty years later.

Bills that, for the entirety of my twenties and thirties, set the parameters for what was financially possible in life, and what wasn't.

Briana and I weren't really keen on renting a place in the city, even before we had kids. We had a dog and a couple of cats. We wanted a bit of yard, maybe someplace to put a grill. We didn't want to be crammed in on top of millions of other people.

So we looked farther afield. Even outside of the cities, however, the economics of home ownership were daunting. In the Baltimore suburbs, which we eventually settled on, a typical detached single-family home goes for somewhere around the same price as a cramped D.C. condo. In 2010, when we were looking, this seemed insane to us: where were people getting the money for these houses? Was everyone in Baltimore an investment banker?

In the end we settled on a 952-square-foot row house on a lot totaling .0359 acres. At the time it was perfect: built of stone in the early 1800s in the mill town of Oella, originally it served as millworkers' quarters. The village was charming and historic (most houses, including our own, didn't receive indoor plumbing until the 1980s) and abutted a state park where the dog could roam.

More important than any of this, however, was the price: $245,000, a relative bargain on account of its old age. Paying a quarter of a million dollars for 952 square feet felt obscene; it was obscene. But by Baltimore/D.C. standards it was a bargain, and in 2010 it was what we could afford.

All that 952 feet of living space was spread across three stories, so we spent a lot of time hiking up and down stairs. We shared walls with neighbors on either side but they were quiet most of the time. Stone walls make for surprisingly poor insulators, so in the winters we heated the place with a pellet stove. In the spring, if you opened a window and listened real hard, you could hear the murmur of the Patapsco River in the valley below.

For a young professional couple with a handful of pets, it was perfect. Then we had the twins.

When we found out we were pregnant—several years after moving into our tiny Oella home—we thought about trying to move to a bigger place. But it was well out of the question. We had nowhere near enough money to make the numbers work.

So we decided to do the best we could with our millworkers' quarters—after all, we reasoned, back in the early 1800s a family would have packed twelve kids into the place. Surely we could find room for two.

And it did work, for a while. While the twins were still babies and mostly immobile. The finished attic became their nursery, with just enough room for two cribs, two dressers, and a rocking chair.

The living room downstairs, meanwhile, could accommodate a double pack-'n'-play for nap times, which along with a love seat for two adults and a wood chair put it at just about maximum capacity. Yes, the pellet stove was in there, but we'd worry about how to block that off once the twins figured out how to move.

But as the twins grew and became mobile it quickly

became apparent that 952 feet wasn't going to cut it any-more. As they approached the year marker it felt as if the house was stuffed to the breaking point with baby paraphernalia. They were trying to crawl and walk, but didn't have a lot of space to figure things out. One after-noon, Charles, trying to master crawling in the tight confines of the living room, instead ended up backing himself fully under the couch. Toys, pillows, stuffed an-imals covered every horizontal surface in the residence. We let the twins crawl around in the dining room for more space, but we had to keep a constant eye out lest one of them squeeze himself through the cat door and tumble down the basement steps.

We needed a bigger place, but we were priced out of the market for a larger home that could accommodate our growing family. We were making decent money, and probably could have convinced a lender to approve a loan of a half million dollars or more if we were ever able to scrounge up a down payment to match. But between child-care costs and the burden of tens of thousands of dollars in student loans, our monthly budget already felt like it was pushed to the breaking point. Taking out more home debt and doubling the size of our monthly mortgage seemed reckless.

Given the demands of our professional lives, time was in short supply as well. My fifteen-hour-a-week com-mute meant that I barely saw the twins at all during the workweek. I was out the door well before they woke up. If I was lucky I'd see them for maybe forty-five minutes in the evening before it was time to put them to bed.

This time wasn't typically quality time, either. It was the end of the day; the twins were tired and cranky because they were two, and that's how two-year-olds are in the evening. Briana was tired and cranky from working a full day at the Social Security Administration and then coming home to deal with the twins by herself for several hours until I made it back. I was tired and cranky from working and being on the train all day.

None of us were at our best between the hours of 6 and 7 p.m. on those weeknights. But that was all the time we had with each other.

The weekends, which we used primarily to recover from the travails of the prior workweek, were not much better. There's a nearly unlimited number of things to do with kids in the Baltimore-D.C. area on a given weekend—take them to the aquarium, or the museums, or the Eastern Shore.

Problem was, of course, that doing just about anything still entailed a lengthy fight with the region's heavy traffic while the twins grew ever more agitated in the backseat. Most activities cost money, which was already in short supply. And the twins had the attention spans of your typical two-year-olds, which meant we'd spend an hour driving somewhere only to have them fuss and fret and complain of boredom and hunger within fifteen minutes of arriving.

So while we were surrounded by the riches the D.C. region had to offer, we typically lacked the time and the energy to enjoy them.

After seven years of living in the D.C. area my health

was bad enough, but the arrival of the twins pushed things over the edge. Shortly after their birth I was beset by a feeling of hopelessness that I now recognize as depression. It had been there most of my adult life, I realized, not terribly severe but always hovering around the margins, waiting to swoop in at inopportune times.

Things had gradually gotten worse during our time in D.C. This, again, isn't a surprise: studies have consistently shown that life in major metropolitan areas is associated with higher rates of mental illness, relative to people who live out in the country.

There's the crime, the pollution, and the paradoxical sense of isolation you experience when surrounded by millions of unsmiling strangers. Where we lived, in a suburb of Baltimore, there was a greater sense of community than in your typical anonymous city. But we were still smack in the heart of a major metropolitan area where it's easy to get lost in an uncaring crowd.

Studies have also consistently shown a link between population density and happiness: the fewer people around you, the more satisfied you are. A study on well-being in Canada found, for instance, that the average population density in the country's 20 percent most miserable communities was more than eight times greater than in the happiest 20 percent of communities.

Surveys in the United States, meanwhile, find that people who live in rural areas are happier than those who live in the suburbs, and suburbanites are happier than city dwellers. Some evolutionary psychologists have proposed a sort of "paleo-happiness" theory to explain this. The human brain, they reason, evolved for life on the African savanna, where our primal ancestors hail from. In that environment you'd find a population density of less than one person per square kilometer. In modern-day Manhattan, by contrast, you've got a population density greater than 27,000 people per square kilometer. Take a brain evolved for the former environment and drop it into the latter and you can see how certain problems might arise.

I'm not sure I completely buy this theory, but it certainly speaks to me on a purely experiential level. The strains of new parenthood, particularly with two children, brought the marginal feelings of dread front and center. I have the twins to thank for being the crisis that finally pushed me to seek help for my depression and treat it with medication. While not a cure-all by any means, the antidepressants I started shortly after their birth helped me keep things in perspective and function like a person unburdened with an irrational sense of dread.

Then there was the blood pressure. Through a stroke of bad genetic luck it's predisposed toward being high—my father had his first stroke at age fifty-six, and doctors had noted with alarm that my numbers were what they called "pre-hypertensive" in my early twenties, in what was otherwise my peak physical fitness.

Years of stressful work, long commutes, and bad eating didn't improve things, and by the time the twins were born my systolic pressure was pushing 150. Time to add another prescription to the regimen.

To cope with all the stress, I was also drinking—a lot. Ten to fifteen drinks per week, maybe? That put me somewhere in the top 20 percent of Americans by alcohol intake. Federal survey data show that binge drinking and heavy alcohol use are more prevalent in urban areas than in rural ones, with evidence of a gradient of use running from the least- to most-populated areas.

In the end, it seems that city life is slowly driving many of us mad. That was the case, at least, for me. Urban life is hazardous to your personal safety, your physical health, and your mental health. Why do we do it? In a word: jobs.

We move to cities that wear us down because that's where the jobs are. Happiness, health, safety—nice things to have, but you need to have a roof over your head before you can even start worrying about them. Historically, city residents have tended to be "well compensated for their joylessness," as one team of economists put it. "The desires for happiness and life satisfaction do not uniquely drive human ambitions," they rather dryly conclude. "Humans are quite understandably willing to sacrifice both happiness and life satisfaction if the price is right."

For many years, in America's cities, the price has been right. But particularly in recent decades the annual return on urban and suburban living has been declining. Rising housing costs and longer commutes have taken big bites out of disposable incomes and the time people have to enjoy them. Wages, meanwhile, have been largely flat for many workers, even those with the best-paying urban jobs.

There's a lot of good things to say about life in a functioning modern metropolis. Economies of scale, access to new people and technologies and ideas—historically the economic case for urbanization has been rooted in ideas like these.

But at what point does present-day urban dysfunction outweigh those economic gains, and even make the return on urbanization negative? What good is it to have a large pool of talented workers if they're all commuting ten hours or more a week? How many mental health days does it take for a modern office worker to achieve equilibrium with the stresses of the modern office?

It had been easier for me to ignore the toll of the commuting lifestyle before the kids were born. The body adapts. If a ninety-minute commute is what it takes to put a roof over your head, then that's what it takes. I would put a good face on it, talk about all the reading I could get done, or all the goofing around on the internet I could do via my phone.

But there's one big piece of evidence that cities aren't all they're cracked up to be: in 2014 the Pew Research Center surveyed Americans on the following question: "If you could live anywhere in the United States that you wanted to, would you prefer a city, a suburban area, a small town or a rural area?"

You might expect that most people answered "city" or "suburbs"—after all, that's where 80 percent of us live. But in fact, given their druthers, more than half of Americans—54 percent, to be exact—say they'd prefer to live in a small town or rural area. Just 24 percent said the city was ideal, and only 21 percent said they'd want to live in a suburb.

The implication is that a considerable chunk of the U.S. population—potentially as much as 30 percent—is stuck in the cities and suburbs and dreaming of escape to the country.

In the summer of 2015 I was one of them.

D.C.'s one redeeming late summer feature is that many of its people are out of town. Congress is on recess, and much of the nation's bureaucratic apparatus—the lobbyists, think tankers, and news media—along with it.

Journalists stuck in D.C. newsrooms in August are often kicking around light, offbeat story ideas that wouldn't see the light of day at other times of year, when there's actual news to write about. This particular context—the lack of real news and the greater tolerance of editors for general dicking around—is important for understanding everything that follows.

Bear in mind, too, that in 2015 the country hadn't yet gone mad over the Trump campaign and eventual presidency; the man was still largely seen as a sideshow, a novelty candidate along the lines of Vermin Supreme, the perennial oddball candidate from Vermont who wears a boot on his head.

What this meant is that readers still had plenty of appetite for quirky, out-of-left-field stories that would take off like social fire on Facebook and Twitter. I just so happened to excel at this sort of story.

In the midst of those August doldrums I happened to see a news release about a Baylor University study finding that people who live in more "beautiful landscapes" are less religious. Apparently it's tough to spend the morning in church when the beach or the mountains call. As a data reporter, however, I was immediately drawn to the independent variable in this scenery-versus-religion equation—how the heck did these guys measure and quantify natural beauty?

As it turns out, a group of data nerds at the U.S. Department of Agriculture did just that in the late 1990s, creating what they called a "natural amenities scale." It all started when the USDA's statisticians were searching for a better understanding of what was driving population change—and more specifically, population decline—in rural areas.

Economic concerns—jobs, again—were a big part of this. But the researchers knew there was another factor at play: the weather. Between 1950 and 2000, for instance, there's a striking correlation between January temperatures and overall population growth in a given city or metropolitan area.

The warmer a place's winters are, in other words, the more people seem to be drawn there. The USDA's researchers reasoned that temperature wasn't the only such amenity. People like interesting landscapes, for instance—craggy peaks and rolling valleys. They like to have water nearby for swimming and boating.

These are the things, in short, that regional tourism boards put in their brochures, or that newcomers call back home to brag about after they arrive. In the end, the researchers arrived at a set of six different measures:

1. Average January temperature (warmer is better)

2. Average January days of sunshine (more is better)

3. Temperate summer, measured as the difference between average temperatures in January and July (a smaller gap is better)

4. Average July humidity (lower is better, for fairly obvious reasons)

5. Topographic variation—hills, valleys, and mountains (more are better)

6. Finally, water area—coastlines and lakes (more are better)

"Natural aspects of attractiveness," as the USDA puts it. They're physical characteristics, products of the landscape and the planetary environment. They're immutable, unchangeable, invulnerable to the machinations of mankind. "Natural amenities pertain to the physical rather than the social or economic environment," the USDA writes. "We can measure the basic ingredients, not how these ingredients have been shaped by nature and man."

The USDA's researchers took all of these measures from existing federal datasets, mashed them together in a statistical blender, and voilà—the natural amenities index was born.

Here's the great thing: there are 3,108 counties in the contiguous United States, according to the Census Bureau. In creating the natural amenities index, the USDA statisticians went ahead and ranked every single one of them according to where they fell on the scale (sadly, Alaska and Hawaii didn't make the cut, in part due to a lack of comparable climatological data for those states).

It was an official federal ranking, in other words, of the lower forty-eight's most beautiful and ugliest places to live.

I pitched the idea of a map based on the index—"a government ranking of the best and worst counties to live in," as I characterized it—to my editors. They gave the thumbs-up, and the rest is the history you're about to read.

The coasts, as it turns out, look pretty good on the natural amenities index, as does much of the mountain west. Ventura County, California, came in at number one on the list—not surprising given the shore, the hills, and the temperate climate. In fact, every single one of the ten highest-ranked counties is located in California.

The county that came in dead last on the list, meanwhile, was a little place I'd never heard of called Red Lake County, Minnesota, which appeared to be far up in the northwest corner of the state.

I had never set foot in Minnesota in my life. So I googled, naturally, which led me to a generic-looking midwestern county government website containing, among other things, a "community calendar" for August that was completely blank.

"Fun fact," the website proudly proclaimed, "it is the only landlocked county in the United States that is surrounded by just two neighboring counties."

Fun!

According to Google, Red Lake County was so far north that in order to get to Fargo from there you'd have to drive two hours south. It was tucked so far away in the middle of nowhere that it was twenty miles from the nearest McDonald's, forty miles from the closest Starbucks, and three hundred miles away from the nearest Whole Foods.

Wikipedia wasn't much help, either. It noted that the county seat was the town of Red Lake Falls, population 1,427. "The last significant historic event in Red Lake Falls occurred on August 27, 1927," Wikipedia's editors noted, "when the famous aviator Charles Lindbergh and his wife landed at the nearby airport during a barnstorming trip through the Upper Midwest and were taken on automobile rides to Huot and Crookston."

Lindbergh, the only famous person to visit the town in the past century, evidently left just as soon as he arrived.

I wanted to add some local color to the story but there simply wasn't much to work with, at least not from my vantage point of a D.C. newsroom. It looked to me like one of those sleepy flyover places that dot the middle of the country, just barely holding on as migration and urbanization slowly whittle its population down to zero.

So I wrote this:

> The absolute worst place to live in America is (drumroll please) . . . Red Lake County, Minn. (claim to fame: "It is the only landlocked county in the United States that is surrounded by just two neighboring counties," according to the county Web site).

And that was it! My first encounter with Red Lake County amounted to just forty-two mildly snarky words, tossed off on a slow Friday afternoon.

The story went up at 9:27 a.m. on Monday morning. By 9:32, the hate mail started rolling in.

It started, as so many unpleasant things do, on Twitter: "As someone who grew up in the heart of 'ugly country' on this map, I hereby declare this map garbage," a Minnesotan named Matt Privratsky wrote.

By midmorning, people who lived in and around Red Lake County started sending me photographs of golden wheat fields, meandering rivers, and deep blue prairie skies. "This is what the 'worst place in America to live in' looks like in late summer," one of them said.

The photographs eventually morphed into a hashtag campaign, #ShowMeYourUglyCounties, inviting Minnesotans to showcase the state's natural beauty and refute claims of a lack of amenities. Many of the responses contained a variant of the word "uffda," an all-purpose Minnesota-ism roughly synonymous with "good grief!"

To be honest, I felt pretty good watching this all unfold from my desk in D.C. People were clicking, reading, and sharing the article, which is just about all most of us in the media asked of our audiences in that era.

One striking thing, however, is that the volume of feedback wasn't accompanied by much vitriol. I write about all sorts of controversial topics, like guns and politics, where even mundane observations can incite frothing rage. There was none of it, though, in the response to the natural amenities story. To the extent that I knew anything about Minnesotans it was that they had a tendency toward humility and politeness, an impression I had gleaned solely from hearing Garrison Keillor on NPR growing up. The weird thing was that, in my first interaction with Minnesotans as a class, they were valiantly living up to their stereotypes.

The other thing: they didn't let up. The social media campaign escalated throughout the day, to the extent that regional news outlets decided to get in on the action.

"Red Lake County was minding its own business," Minneapolis alternative newspaper *City Pages* wrote. "Then out of the blue prairie skies some East Coast media type with a hogwash government index calls the swath of northwest Minnesota 'the absolute worst place to live in America.'"

That reporter called up county commissioner Charles Simpson to ask what he thought of the fracas. "What they've got to say, it's bullshit," he said.

The *Star Tribune* subsequently asked Simpson what he thought of me, personally, for their own story. "He can kiss my butt," Simpson said.

By this time the story had received wide enough traction that then-senator Al Franken weighed in. "You're totally right @washingtonpost—Red Lake County has no natural beauty," he wrote in a sarcastic Twitter post accompanied by a bucolic photo of the county's Old Crossing Treaty Park. Tagging my employer's account in that tweet was a nice touch, ensuring that our social media team were aware of the abuse Minnesotans were facing in my careless hands.

I want to pause for a minute here to point out something interesting. If you go back to the original map, you'll see that it's not just northwest Minnesota—there are a lot of places in the United States that don't look good on the USDA's index. The North Dakota side of the Red River Valley fared just as poorly, as did a wide swath of the rust belt region running down through Iowa, Illinois, and up through Ohio.

I didn't hear a single word of complaint from any of these states, though. Not even one. No indignant Iowans. No outraged North Dakotans. I did, however, receive an email from a resident of Nebraska. He had noticed that his region of the state didn't look good on the map, and had considered lodging a complaint. But the more he thought about it, he told me, the more he felt he agreed with the ranking. "I guess Omaha really is kind of a dump," he said.

I must have written dozens of similar pieces to this in

the course of a career—find a dataset, map it out, call out the highs and lows, and call it a day. But I had never received a torrent of feedback from a low-ranking locality like I did from Minnesotans that August.

In fact, there's a phrase among statisticians: "Thank God for Mississippi." The idea is that in just about any state-level ranking of a given quantity—whether it be economic, demographic, cultural, social, or anything else—Mississippi usually ends up at the very bottom of the list. If you're from, say, Alabama, that's something to be thankful for.

I've done an awful lot of stories where Mississippi ends up at the bottom of some ranking or another. And again, I don't believe I've ever heard a single word of complaint from a Mississippi resident. Minnesotans were a different breed entirely.

In a lighthearted attempt at amends-making, I rounded up a bunch of the best responses to the original article and published them in a follow-up piece several days later titled "Thick Coats, Thin Skins: Why Minnesotans Were Outraged by a Recent *Washington Post* Report."

For the piece I asked one of the original instigators, Matt Privratsky, what his deal was. "Minnesotans are known for being very humble and even reserved," he said, "but as this reaction shows we're also very proud of our state—especially when in competition with those around us."

If Red Lake County wasn't the ugliest place in the nation, what was? "I wouldn't be doing my job as a born and bred Minnesotan if I didn't tell people to avoid Wisconsin," Privratsky wrote.

Later in the week I got an email with the subject line "An invitation to come visit Red Lake County." It was from a guy named Jason Brumwell. His family, he wrote, owned a river tubing business based in the town of Red Lake Falls. "I would like to cordially and officially invite you to come and check out our little county which has now been dubbed, 'The Worst County in the United States,'" he said. Citing the online criticism that had been going on, he said that "I would also like to reassure you that you would be given plenty of good natured 'ribbing' but would be greeted with open arms and a lot of people showing you why they feel our county is far from the worst."

Hmmm.

The first thing I did after reading the email several times over in search of obvious signs of mental instability was to google Brumwell and his business, Voyageur's View. Everything seemed to be on the up-and-up. The Francophile spelling was an interesting touch—a nod, as it turned out, to the French explorers who played a major role in settling the region in the 1600s and 1700s.

I have to admit that at this point I was plenty curious to see what the place was actually like—to get the view from the ground, rather than from a spreadsheet. I had never been to Minnesota; in fact I'd never really even spent any time in the Midwest.

When Briana got home that evening I told her about the email and asked her what she thought. I should point out that even under the best circumstances my job was a source of anxiety for her, given the torrents of vitriol I'd often stir up in the comments section of my stories and on social media.

"So, a guy out there wants me to come and visit," I told her.

Her eyes grew wide. "Oh my God, they're going to kill you aren't they," she said.

"Come on, no," I said. "You saw how polite everyone was. This guy seems really nice; there's like seven exclamation points in his email."

"So they're gonna what, tar and feather you instead? It's a trap. Don't do it."

It took some convincing but I finally got Briana on board with the idea. My editors were easier to convince. In fact, they were suspiciously enthusiastic about the idea. "D.C. Reporter Gets Tarred, Feathered by Indignant Minnesotans" would be a nice story to end the summer with.

At any rate, a few days later I was on a plane headed to the North Star State. It was time to experience Red Lake County firsthand.

Getting there, it turned out, was a bit of a challenge. Red Lake Falls is so far out of the way that the closest "major" airport (with just two gates) is in Grand Forks, North Dakota—an hour away and across the state line. As I flew in for my visit, the view out the airplane window was a rigid grid, straight roads stretching out to the horizon interrupted only by other straight roads running perpendicularly. Everything was flat, square. It certainly looked like it could be America's worst place to live.

I did some reading before I left to find out what kind of place I'd be parachuting into. By most economic metrics, the county seemed to be doing okay. The unemployment rate that July was 4.6 percent, well below the national average. The median household income was $48,000—less than half the typical income in the Washington suburbs.

The median home value, on the other hand, was just $89,000, or one-fifth the typical home price where I was living. That works out to a home price to income ratio of about two-to-one—a hell of a lot more favorable than D.C.'s eight-to-one ratio.

The county was home to just a hair over four thousand people, 95 percent of whom were white. The median age of 42.1 was about five years greater than the U.S. average. Overall the county's population density was ten people per square mile—approximately 99 percent less dense than Baltimore County, Maryland.

The big business in the county was farming—more than three hundred farms, according to the U.S. Census of Agriculture. In terms of landscape it was 80 percent farmland, 10 percent forest, and 7 percent grassland. Just 1.6 percent of the land area was devoted to towns and residences. It was home to approximately twice as many cows as people.

A picture was starting to emerge in my head of a place older, whiter, sparser and struggling—I imagined it not wholly unlike the hardscrabble farming communities that surrounded the town of Oneonta, New York, where I had grown up. People in the "big city" of Oneonta (pop. 13,000) looked down on these other communities, and I had been no different. We thought of them as hicks.

Secretly, though, I had always been fascinated by these places. In high school I dated a number of girls— Briana was one of them—from these strange, small towns. I was struck above all by a sense of familiarity among the people who lived there. The kids, for instance, seemed to move around these towns as if the entire place belonged to them. They would enter stores and have long conversations with the people behind the counter, or hang out at the schools long after the closing bells, striding confidently along the halls like they had the keys to the place.

It wasn't like that in Oneonta. Boundaries between places you were and weren't supposed to be were strictly policed. People were more anonymous and you didn't know everyone. The town was full of strangers, which is a key difference between a place with 13,000 people and one with 1,300. Social science literature talks a lot about third places, like coffee shops and libraries, that serve as community focal points. Places not home, and not work or school, where people can gather and feel like they belong. In the small communities outside Oneonta it seemed to me that the entire towns were third places for many of the people who lived there. In Oneonta, by contrast, it felt like there weren't any. More often than not, kids who were bored after school would end up at the local Wal-Mart with a group of friends, seeing what kind of trouble they could get into.

Jason Brumwell was extremely enthusiastic about the visit. Ahead of my arrival he sent me an email detailing the plans he was making—lining up people to talk about why they stay; even in "mid winter when it's 40 below zero we have six hours of sunlight . . . there are so many people who want to show you so many things that I'll try and narrow it down so you can take in the best of the best and we'll cover more when you inevitably want to come back again!" I was skeptical, to say the least.

He closed his missive by offering to put me up at his house and warning me to prepare for "a huge helping of Minnesota nice!" The email contained nineteen sentences, twelve of which ended in an exclamation point.

Jason told me to meet him at the county courthouse in Red Lake Falls once I arrived. "Some of the community actually wanted to greet you," he explained. I rented a car from the rental desk at the airport, which was near a large, possibly military-grade lawn mower on display from a local retailer. A scale model of a drone hung from the ceiling, an evident nod to the University of North Dakota's aviation program.

I drove through the city of Grand Forks, crossed the Red River marking the border between North Dakota and Minnesota, and hit the upper midwestern prairie roads for the first time. At Jason's suggestion I took the "back way," a county highway traversing the forty miles of nothing between East Grand Forks and Red Lake Falls.

What struck me first wasn't the flatness or the emptiness or the complete lack of people or cars anywhere within my field of view—it was the sky. Unencumbered by hills and valleys, the sky seemed impossibly vast to my east coast eyes that afternoon, a clear blue dome dotted by plump, poofy clouds straight out of a children's book. The horizon was truly infinite, the sense of scale and space and openness almost humbling.

Agricultural fields vectored off in every direction. The road I was on shot eastward indefinitely, crossed every mile by dirt roads running north and south, bearing well-ordered names: 170th Street, 160th Street, and so on. It was vast but tidy.

At one point I pulled my car over to the side of the road to take pictures and ended up standing there for a few minutes, luxuriating in the silence. The only sounds were the occasional bird chirp rising above the rustle of the wind through cornstalks.

As I approached Red Lake Falls some unexpected variation presented itself—after twenty-two miles of straight-arrow eastward driving, the first turn. As I got even closer to town the road veered south, and then dipped down a small valley toward what a sign proclaimed to be the Red Lake River, the county's namesake.

Crossing the river I saw the sign for Jason Brumwell's business, Voyageur's View Camping and Tubing, overlooking a wide swath of mowed grass leading to a collection of red-roofed wood buildings.

Passing the campground the road broadened as I entered the town of Red Lake Falls proper, demarcated by a large wooden sign that proclaimed "Welcome to Red Lake Falls" over a background that suggested mountains and lakes, rather incongruously given the flat agricultural landscape. A large, handcarved wooden loon was propped up against one of the sign legs.

I drove past tidy homes with trim, tightly cropped lawns, the domestic counterpart to the orderly fields outside town. There was what appeared to be a bar, T&J's, on one side of the road, standing next to an evidently vacant building that resembled nothing so much as an old bank.

Turning onto the town's main drag, the first order of business was crossing a large sloped bridge over another river, the Clearwater. Looking down the riverway I saw a series of large chalky cliffs rising fifty feet or so above the water. They offered just the slightest hint of the stark, arid landscape of the Dakotas, a reminder that the region stands at the border between the forests of the east and the more dramatic landscapes of the west.

I found the courthouse—not difficult, given that it was the largest building in town—parked the car, and didn't even manage to get the door all the way open before I was surprised by a microphone in my face. It was a member of the local media, asking me what I was doing and how I liked the place so far and what my plans were for the next few days. I did my best to answer his questions before an older gentleman pulled me aside. I noticed he was wearing a Voyageur's View shirt.

"Are you Jason?" I asked.

"No, I'm his dad, Dick," he said. "Jason's over there," he added, gesturing toward the courthouse. At this point I was able to take in the scene for the first time.

There weren't just a "handful" of people waiting to meet me, as Jason had suggested—there were dozens. There were camera crews, four or five of them. I heard music—there was a color guard from the local high school in full uniform, arrayed along the courthouse steps and striking up a patriotic tune.

Dick led me over to a guy about my age with a thick layer of facial scruff and a Minnesota Twins hat, sipping from an energy drink. This must be Jason. I noticed then that the air was thick with yellowjackets, and that a number of them kept trying to crawl into the drink can. He was swatting them away absentmindedly.

We greeted each other, then Jason took a swig from his can and made an odd face. "Oh, I think I just swallowed one," he said nonchalantly. There was a certain odd forwardness to the "oh" that made him sound like an extra from *Fargo*, the Coen Brothers movie.

We stood there in awkward silence for a few minutes to watch the band play its number. I was quite literally dumbstruck, slowly grappling with the full realization that at this point I was less reporting a story than becoming one myself. I quietly fretted over whether I'd get in trouble with my editors for creating a stir.

Jason led me inside the courthouse. Given the amount of media interest, the locals thought it best I sit down with the reporters for an impromptu press conference before getting on with the day's business.

I knew they'd probably be expecting a snooty east coaster, so I tried to answer their questions with some humility and gee-whizzedness to play against type. I told them about the nice emails I had received from Minnesota people, the response from politicians, and my wife's misgivings. I tried to frame the whole thing as a useful refresher on the limitations of viewing the world through a spreadsheet—limitations that would be obvious to a normal person, but easy for someone in my position to lose track of.

After that I chatted with the town's mayor, Kevin Harmoning, and city administrator Kathleen Schmitz. I asked them about the biggest challenges facing the town, hoping for something juicy—crime? Meth? Crippling poverty?

No, it was "just making ends meet," Harmoning said, referring to keeping the town running, the bills paid, and the lights on. During the recession, they had actually been forced to turn some of the streetlights off to keep everything else running, Schmitz said. But all in all, the downturn's effects hadn't been as harsh here as elsewhere. Many of the farms outside of town that form the economic backbone of the county weren't affected much at all. "People still needed to eat," Schmitz said.

It reminded me of what a social studies teacher had told me way back in high school, back in upstate New York. The class had been talking about economics, of booms and recessions, and how neither one of those things ever seemed to affect the small towns the way they did the cities. "We don't get the highs and we don't get the lows," he had said. "But we always do pretty much okay." I had thought at the time that there was some comfort in that. After eight years of living in the D.C. area, hearing similar thoughts delivered in a county courthouse 1,400 miles away gave me a pang of homesickness.

From the courthouse, Brumwell and his dad loaded me and a gaggle of reporters and local luminaries onto roofless red tour bus—one of the fleet they used to ferry tubers to the river launch—and took us to a dairy farm outside of town owned by brothers Carl and Joe Schindler. They milk about 120 cows 12 at a time the old-fashioned way, with a simple pump system installed in their dairy barn.

Unbeknownst to my hosts, I had had some experience with dairy farms growing up. My dad, the large animal veterinarian, saw a lot of dairy cows. For several summers in my childhood in upstate New York I would ride around on farm calls with him in lieu of day care or any other more structured and costly activity. I had come to know and love the sensory overload of a working dairy farm—the hot, earthy pungency of the manure, the lowing of the cows, the odd combination of astringency and liquid warmth in the dairy parlor.

It had been ages since I had pet a cow, though, and I couldn't wait to do it again. I bounded off the bus as soon as we stopped and made my way over to the calf pens. A newborn calf suckled my thumb as the brothers told me about life on the farm. The earthy smells of a dairy operation—manure and hay and sawdust and dirt—hung thick in the air.

Carl asked if I wanted to check out the inside of the barn and yes, of course I did. We walked around back and into it, chatting a bit more as the huge industrial fans did their best to move the hot midwestern August air around. A member of one of the camera crews tried to follow us in for some footage but ended up retching near the entry of the barn, overcome by the smell.

"I'm really impressed you're in here, actually," Carl said. I told him about my dairy experiences growing up. "Smells great to me," I said. "Smells like home."

Carl's story was similar to what I'd heard at city hall. Yes, life was challenging. A lot of the dairy farms had closed up shop years ago, victims of the relentless trend toward bigger and more high-tech operations that was happening all over the agricultural industry. Red Lake County wasn't immune to any of this. In the 1950s, for instance, there were close to one thousand active farms in the county, according to USDA data. But by 2012 the number had fallen by more than half, and their average acreage had roughly doubled. Fewer farms means fewer families: the population of the county fell from 6,805 people in 1950 to just a hair over 4,000 people in 2012.

But Carl and his brother were still here, and despite their small size they were doing okay. Five years, ten years down the line? Who could tell. But for now the numbers added up.

I found myself thinking of Jack and Charles as we

toured the property, petting calves and feeding hay to the lumbering heifers. Wouldn't it be great for them to grow up in a place where they could have this kind of experience? There was a petting zoo fairly close to home in Maryland that we had visited several times. The disinterested animals did their best to avoid the crowds of kids always running around the place; they'd seek out the shady corners of their enclosures to escape the sweltering Maryland summer sun. My own kids would quickly tire of competing with others for the attention of a stray goat and would be clamoring for snacks and other diversions within fifteen minutes of arrival.

After the farm, the next activity was a chance to reckon with the reality of the Red Lake County landscape via a kayak ride down the Red Lake River. I was prepared to be underwhelmed. On the bus ride over to the kayak launch, I learned that there were no lakes in Red Lake County—the name derived from the Red Lake River, which in turn was named after its source, the Red Lake, a massive body of fresh water about fifty miles east of the county.

"What about the falls?" I asked.

"What falls?" Jason said.

"Red Lake Falls?"

"Oh, there aren't any falls in Red Lake Falls."

"So there's neither a lake, nor falls, in the town of Red Lake Falls?"

"Nope," he said.

Still, you can't complain about an afternoon kayak

trip on work time. We got to the launch and Jason shoved me off onto the river in the company of four locals.

Our boats glided silently under an old railroad trestle. The tracks above had been converted to a paved trail some years back, my companions told me. As we rounded the river bend we came to the brick shell of a power station that used to sit on the river. Someone mentioned it would be a perfect place to convert to a riverside dining establishment, and it was hard to disagree.

The river wasn't particularly large, maybe just ten kayak widths across. In the Northeast any river of this size tends to be shallow and rocky, but this one was tranquil, carving deep meanders through the landscape as it went. Dusty cliffs rose up on one side and then the other, pocked with holes where swallows nested. It felt like a western river but on miniature scale.

At one point one of my companions, a woman named Melissa Benoit, surreptitiously pulled out her phone and played the dueling-banjos theme from *Deliverance*. Melissa was a Red Lake Falls gal roughly my age; she'd moved around the country a bit after high school and ended up settling down back here, where friends and family were. She knew I'd probably been expecting a bunch of toothless rednecks and figured she'd have some fun at my expense. And indeed, to my surprise there was nothing about the place that suggested redneckery. The homes visible from the riverside were well kept, tidy. The rural areas of upstate New York where I grew up had a different feel to them—houses were often ramshackle, lawns over-grown with chunks of old cars or faded playground equipment strewn about. There was none of that here. The word that kept popping into my head was "tidy." The area conveyed a sense of quiet, working-class normalcy.

Two of our other companions were a ten-year-old boy named Jayce, a student at the local elementary school, and his grandfather. Like many kids in the area Jayce was wild about hockey. Because the region was so sparsely populated, teams, even elementary school ones, would sometimes travel two, three, even four hours for the sake of a hockey match.

Jayce also gave me a sense of how the locals viewed themselves vis-à-vis Minneapolis, the state's largest city, some five hours to the south. Jayce said he'd been there with his family and didn't care much for it.

"Why?" I asked.

"There's cars everywhere," he said. "And the people are crazy-looking!"

I found that people up here spoke of Minneapolis the same way upstate New Yorkers talk about New York City—a far-off urban hellscape populated by millions of strange people who manage to draw a disproportionate share of attention and state resources. This was odd for me, since as a lifelong east coaster I'd always imagined Minneapolis as a sort of charming little hobbit village, full of farmer's markets and artisanal craft stores.

Our tour ended at a place known to locals as the Point, where the Red Lake meets the Clearwater at a park in town. I hitched a ride back to my rental car with Jason, and then stopped by my motel room to check in and get a shower before dinner, which was evidently to be open to the public, at T&J's.

My lodgings were at the Chateau Motel & Liquor Store, which is exactly what it sounds like: a regular roadside motel with a liquor store attached to it. Everything a weary traveler needs. As I fired off a few texts to Briana, letting her know I was safe and untarred, I noticed I had literally dozens of Facebook notifications. I opened the app to find that they were nearly all friend requests from Minnesotans I had met earlier in the day. Minnesota Nice, indeed.

The folks at T&J's were outgoing and eager to talk about what made their community so special. Al Buse, for instance, was Red Lake Falls' oldest resident at 101— "like everyone's grandpa," Jason told me. He was the grandson of one of the town's original founders. He still lived alone, in a house on Main Street that was a veritable history museum—photographs and memorabilia of the town's history, and, naturally, an arsenal of firearms stored in the basement.

Al, it seemed, was the living, breathing avatar of the sense of civic pride and duty that made the town of Red Lake Falls tick. In the summers when the weather was nice, every morning he would load his tools in the back of his bright yellow golf cart and make his way through town, fixing things that need fixing, watering plants, generally doing whatever he could to keep the town, well, tidy.

For dessert, the restaurant served a cake built as a map of the county by baking prodigy Matt Weiss, a local high school student. I helped myself to the Red Lake Falls portion of the cake.

"See all these other little towns?" Jason said, pointing to places on the cake labeled Brooks, Oklee, and Plummer. "That's where we're going tomorrow."

Jason had procured a tour bus from his friend Jesse, the guy who owned T&J's. They had decked it out for the occasion, with a sign reading "America's Worst Tour" splayed above the windshield. He had also invited a number of luminaries from the county's four major towns to accompany us.

We visited a wheat farm in Brooks (pop. 139), where fourth-generation farmer Alex Yaggie, twenty-seven, showed me the cockpit of one of his forty-foot combines and let me drive it around an empty lot as much as I dared. We stopped at an asparagus farm outside Red Lake Falls, the first of its kind in the region, and sampled from a fiercely flavorful jar of pickled asparagus.

We stopped for lunch—fried cheese curds and a "Minnesota burger"—at T.J.'s Tavern in the town of Oklee (pop. 418). U.S. representative Collin Peterson, a Minnesota Democrat, swung by and sang an ode to ugliness on the bar's main stage. Ugly women in particular, something he probably wouldn't have done in our current post-#MeToo era.

We stopped at the Plummer Area Sportsmen's Club, where county commissioner Chuck Simpson—the gruff fellow who'd given such spicy quotes to Minneapolis media about my original story—showed me around the shooting range.

By the end of the day I was worn out from all the glad-handing. It was a good kind of worn out, though. Over and over, the folks I spoke with told me it was that sense of community that kept them here and contributed to that enormous outpouring of civic pride in response to my original article. "There's lots of freedom here," Jason Brumwell told me later that night, at a barbecue at his dad's house. "But everybody's still watching out for each other."

CHAPTER 2

The next day, following my whirlwind tour of Red Lake County, I packed my bags and flew back to Baltimore, to Briana, the twins, and the job. I had plenty to think about on the flight back home.

The trip had been a jarring break in the well-worn routine I'd established for myself in D.C. and Baltimore. It cast the shortcomings of our family's situation in a jarring light. When I told people in Red Lake Falls about the length of my commute, for instance, their jaws dropped. I realized I had built up a protective layer of apathy around myself that allowed me to ignore the steep cost of the big commute, the small house, the disconnect among the crowds, all of it. After all, it was simply something that everyone did, on some level or another, out in D.C.

And yet, Red Lake County—and other places like it— were filled with people whose lives were radically different. They had space. Yards. Breathing room. Small communities where people knew and looked after one another. The very existence of Red Lake County and the people who lived there was a direct challenge to the way of life we had slid into in the city. It undermined the inevitability of modern urban life.

Like many people on the coasts, I had a foggy notion

that places like Red Lake County were out there. We all knew about the rural-urban divide in the United States. But I had previously thought of rural places as fundamentally other, strange lands where unfamiliar people held tight to ancient customs and beliefs. Even though I grew up in upstate New York, after a decade in D.C. a rural midwestern farming community seemed about as remote and foreign to me as an Amish enclave, or an Amazonian tribe that hadn't yet made contact with modern society.

But the most earth-shattering revelation of my trip had been this: the people in Red Lake County were just like the rest of us. They watched the same TV shows, followed the same news, consumed the same popular culture, and cracked the same dumb jokes. I went out there expecting to find a tribe of people who were radically different but instead I was shocked to find out they were just like me. How, then, had I ended up wasting my life in a cramped town house, riding a cramped train, while they got to enjoy the clean prairie air and the wide-open spaces of northwest Minnesota? Why couldn't I be more like them? Where had I gone wrong?

Back at the grind in D.C., my days in Red Lake County took on a positively Norman Rockwellian cast. While there I had relentlessly poked and prodded the people I talked to, puzzled by the optimism, the pride, the sense of belongingness. "Yes, but what about all the bad stuff?" I asked. What about the drugs? The crippling poverty? The squalor and misery of a benighted life in the countryside?

Yet no matter how hard I pushed, I couldn't find any sign of rot beneath the region's bucolic exterior. The people had their trials and headaches, of course. Downtown Red Lake Falls wasn't what it had once been. Affordable health care was a challenge. The sheriff's office had the occasional speeder or shoplifter to deal with.

But while the rural communities I had known as a child seemed to be almost devoured by their challenges, the people in Red Lake Falls were rising up to meet theirs. There the pressures of modern life seemed manageable, in a way that they must have seemed across the entire nation in say, the 1950s and 1960s. I wanted that manageability in my own life. I wanted to take my family to a place where it didn't feel like the trend lines of time and money were always converging, squeezing us into an ever-narrowing sphere of existence. I wanted to turn the trends around, set them outward and away from each other, opening up wide spaces of possibility with room to breathe. I wanted what the people in Red Lake County seemed to have.

I wrote my follow-up story on my visit, closing it with these lines: "When people and places halfway across the country are just a mouse-click away on your computer, it's easy to assume that we live in a nation made small and manageable by technology. But traveling to a place like Red Lake County, hours away from any major metro area, is a reminder that in much of the country, the rhythms of daily life are, still, markedly different than the coastal city grind of long commutes and high-octane jobs.

"For some of us, it takes a place as small as Red Lake County to drive home just how big this country really is."

As I got back into the D.C. grind I found myself unable to shake the memories of the trip. Jammed into a hot, overcrowded Red Line train, I thought of the guy I'd talked to in Plummer who complained about how sometimes getting stuck behind a tractor would add five minutes to his fifteen-minute commute.

Wading through diesel fumes on the streets of D.C., crowded in by the city's squat, blocky buildings, I would have given just about anything for five more minutes on a dirt road out on the prairie, hemmed in by nothing but a warm breeze.

I dreamed about the people I had met, nothing crazy, just about running into them and chatting them up at the store.

My wife noticed a change in my demeanor when I returned. I am not exactly what you'd call a people person. I'm a natural introvert; given the choice between socializing with others or doing something by myself, I'll nearly always choose the latter. There's a reason why I spend most of my reporting time interrogating datasets, rather than people.

The running joke in the Ingraham household is that Briana is a normal, functioning social adult while I am "dead inside." Yet when I came back from Minnesota, Briana noticed that I wouldn't stop talking about how great the people were. Their warmth, their friendliness, their fiercely held determination to make their communities better. Even for an introvert it was striking to see.

I contrasted that with what I had known from the neighborhoods I had lived in. In our early twenties Briana and I spent a particularly miserable year in grad school in Southern California, living in a corporate-managed apartment complex that catered mostly to low-income families. The apartments were crammed in on top of each other and it was impossible to escape the sight, sound, or smell of your neighbors at any hour of the day or night. But nobody talked to one another—everyone kept their heads down, desperate to avoid having to humanize the people you knew only as, say, the source of the music that blared every weeknight at 11 p.m., or the arguments you could hear through your paper-thin walls.

We had lived in Vermont for a couple years shortly thereafter—our initial goal in relocating there was simply to put as much space between us and Southern California as we could manage. But New Englanders, as we discovered, are not known for their openness to outsiders. We were able to find nonsqualid rental accommodations and managed to make a couple of close friends there. But the communities we lived in, outside of Burlington, made zero effort to help residents get to know each other, or to develop a sense of community identity beyond the occasional appeal to NIMBYism whenever someone wanted to install a new windmill or power line.

After Briana got recruited to work for the Social Security Administration, we moved to the Baltimore area and came to like it much more than we thought we would. We settled in the historic district of Ellicott City, a charming collection of shops and restaurants tucked away into brick and stone-crafted buildings. The historic district had something of an identity of its own, but its location in the middle of one of the east coast's largest metropolitan areas tended to dilute that. It was also marred by a busy connecting road that cut right through the middle of the district, essentially shoving the town's civic life to the margins of the roadway.

We made a number of friends when we moved to Oella, many of whom were struggling with the same issues we were—how to raise children in a cramped, pedestrian-hostile space? How to pay bills without burning most of your nonworking hours on interminable trips to D.C.?

That fall Briana and I were coming to the realization that we had to do something about our current situation. It was killing us, in both a metaphoric and also a very literal sense. The problem was that no matter how hard we tried, no matter how far outside the box we started to think, we couldn't make the numbers add up.

We looked into selling our home and renting a place closer to D.C. The problem was there was no way to increase our square footage without drastically raising our monthly housing costs, and even then we'd be stuck on the fringes of some dodgy area like Laurel or Odenton, almost certainly living in cramped, factory-style quarters like we'd done in California. The only difference now would be even higher rent, and we'd have kids to manage to boot.

We looked at going in the other direction—what if we moved waaay out to the fringes, to the very farthest reaches of where the MARC train traveled? Make peace with the long commute, embrace it even. Live in say, Harpers Ferry, West Virginia, and cajole the bosses to let me work from home two days a week. The problem was that unless we got way out into the boonies—like six-hour-a-day commute instead of three—the home prices were still insane. Even in the easternmost reaches of West Virginia, a $300,000 single-family home is a rarity.

The truth is that that phrase—single-family home—meant little to me before the kids came along. I had absorbed and understood all the urban-lefty critiques of single-family home ownership that are so prevalent on the coast: high-density living, in condos and apartments and town homes, is better for the environment. It fosters interpersonal communication, and creates urban spaces better suited for humans than for cars.

But I had come to suspect that much of the urbanist critique of single-family home ownership was really a critique of *suburban* single-family homeownership. My time in Southern California had certainly illustrated the limits of the "planned community." Despite the "master plan" governing Irvine and much of Orange County, the area was still a riotously unpleasant place to live. The landscape was shredded into pieces by heavily trafficked roadways, a necessity due to zoning regulations mandating that the places where people worked, gathered, played, and shopped be rigidly separated from the places where they lived.

The suburbs' pitch, in theory, is that they offer the best of both possible worlds: reasonable proximity to urban centers with all their options for work and play, with a little bit of space to stretch out in and call your own. In reality, I began to suspect, many suburbs were just offering the worst: high-density, high-traffic neighborhoods rivaling the most congested urban areas, wedded to rural notions of car ownership and resource consumption.

After the kids arrived I wanted that single-family home. I wanted the yard, the space, the lack of neighbors sharing walls. But I didn't want the suburban version. I didn't want Southern California, or Columbia, Maryland. I didn't want a city, or a suburb. I wanted a town. A village. Hell, a house in the country miles away from anything, I didn't care. Whatever its faults, the town I grew up in, Oneonta, New York, was like this. We lived in a medium-sized house on a main road at the west end of town. There was an auto body shop on one side of us and a Dunkin' Donuts on another. Just down the block and off the main road lay the quiet residential neighborhood where most of my friends lived growing up. We had free rein of the place pretty much as soon as we were old enough to pedal a bike. We played hide-and-seek in the cemetery, built forts in the adjacent woods, biked to the nearby Ames to buy candy, and terrorized the servers at our local Ponderosa. It was a childhood that was completely unremarkable, except for the fact that anything like it now appeared to be unobtainable anywhere within one hundred miles of a typical city.

I wanted that kind of childhood for my own kids, which is another way of saying that I wanted them to have that kind of childhood for myself. I wanted to live in a place where the economic, physical, legal, and cultural conditions all came together to make it possible: affordable homes. Reasonable commutes. Neighborhood spaces where you could walk, play, explore, get lost, maybe even get into a bit of trouble. Adults not accustomed to calling the cops every time they saw a kid unattended. Enough people to look out for one another, but not so many that crime was an issue.

As I was working through these issues, Briana was getting burnt out at work. She spent day after day in meetings and on conference calls, talking around in circles with career bureaucrats who seemed to be checking off time until they collected their pension. She wanted to make things better, but the federal bureaucracy didn't make it easy.

She'd get home exhausted at the end of the day and hear about all the wonderful things Jack and Charles had done with Heather, the nanny. Jack took his first steps. Charles said his first words. They went to the park, to the aquarium, to McDonald's. Milestone after milestone passed by, hours and days of priceless early childhood bonding outsourced to a third party while we labored to keep a roof over our heads, memories left unmade while Briana sat in conference rooms and drafted emails.

Early childhood is another realm where Americans have grown accustomed to going against their own best wishes in the name of paying the bills. In 2016 the Pew Research Center reported that about 60 percent of Americans said children were typically better off with a parent at home. This belief cut across political as well as gender divides, with majorities of nearly every demographic group holding it. Yet in close to half of two-parent households, both parents work full-time.

The actual research into the question of whether kids are better or worse off when both parents work is mostly a wash. To the extent that any effects are observed, they appear to stem from far more fundamental questions: if life at home is safe and stable and generally free from economic woes, the kids are probably going to be all right.

But the research has less to say on the nonquantifiable aspects of early child-rearing: how do you assign a value to the hugs missed, the boo-boos unkissed, the songs unsung, and the experiences unshared? Most of us don't become parents in order to celebrate the outcomes tracked by economists and developmental psychologists: the endgame of parenthood isn't a 90th percentile PSAT score or an above-average place in the national earnings distribution.

Rather we do it for more primal, fundamental reasons: biological necessity. The thrill of creating a new life. The human experience in all its agony and glory. Perhaps above all, love.

Yet those are the very things we deprive ourselves of when we outsource child-rearing to a third party.

Briana and I were both feeling that loss acutely. What if, instead of moving, one of us quit work to be home with the kids? What if we reclaimed that full experience of parenthood? To actually be there to watch our sons grow up?

Yet again, the math didn't add up. Our salaries were similar at the time, which meant that regardless of who left work, our income would be halved. Yes, the childcare expenses would disappear, too, but it wouldn't make up for the forgone income. Between the mortgage, student loans, and various credit card debts incurred in the first expensive years of the boys' lives, one income in the D.C. area was simply out of the question.

We were back at square one.

It was October, and by this point the answer was practically staring us in the face, although we didn't realize it yet. And we wouldn't, until one long weekend when my mom and stepdad flew in from Tampa to visit their grandsons.

The boys were in bed and the four adults were unwinding in our tiny living room, glasses of wine in hand. Seating-wise that room accommodated little beyond a two-person love seat—my mom was sitting on a footstool, and I was squatting on the floor.

Briana and I were talking through all these issues—the boys, the house, the jobs, the commutes, and how we couldn't find a way out of any of it. In the end, my mom was the first one to come right out and say it: "Well, what if you moved to that nice little Minnesota town Chris visited over the summer?"

We all laughed.

"No, really," she said.

The room went quiet.

For me, in that moment, suddenly all the pieces fell in place. One of us would work from home. The other would take a break to be with the kids, which we could afford given the low cost of living. We could get a bigger, cheaper home. There would be no more commute.

"I don't know," I said, suddenly. "Maybe this idea is—"

"Ridiculous," Bri said suddenly. "Who moves to northwest Minnesota?"

"No, wait," I said. "Let's talk about this."

"We're gonna, what?" she asked. "Buy a house in the ugliest county in America?"

"I mean . . . it's not like we have a lot of other options at the moment."

"Mm-hmm. And how cold does it get there in the winter?"

"Uh . . ."

This had the potential to be a problem. I don't mind the cold but Briana is notoriously pro-heat and cold-averse. A big part of the reason that Red Lake County, the place, became Red Lake County, America's worst place, was its bone-chilling winter cold. I prevaricated.

"Maybe it gets like, a *little* bit colder than upstate New York," I admitted.

"Forget about the stupid cold!" my mom said, coming

to my rescue. "Buy some sweaters, for Christ's sake, who cares. Think about the time you'd have with the boys! Think about raising them among all those nice people you said you met there."

"It's true," I said. "I hate most people, but those were some of the best people I've ever met. You'd love them, Bri."

Bri raised an eyebrow. I realized this could be a fruitful line of persuasion.

"Now, wait a minute, just how cold are we talking?" my stepdad interjected. Goddammit, Jeff, I thought.

"Cold winters, warm hearts," I said, sounding like an idiot.

"How are we going to work out there in the middle of nowhere?" Bri asked.

"I can work remotely," I said, not sure if I actually could. "It's the perfect place—the *Post* will want a correspondent in Real America for the election year. And you won't have to work at all!"

"I'm not sure if I want to not have to work at all," she said.

She had started building her career when we lived in Vermont, first as a disability adjudicator with the state's Social Security office (we both applied for the job shortly after moving; she was the one who got it). From there she was recruited to the home office in D.C. and worked her way up to the front office, where all the big policy decisions were made. Despite everything she hated about it, by 2015 her career was a big part of her identity. She liked making more money than either of her parents did. She liked having an identity independent of her husband, her kids, or the rest of her family. The job was a pain in the ass, yes, but it was also independence, financial security, a seat at the world's table.

Now she was supposed to throw all that away and what, move to a tiny midwestern farming community, sight unseen?

We didn't make any decisions that night. But over the next few days, as we intermittently talked it over, the plan—if there was going to be any plan—gradually came into focus. It would obviously make the most sense for me to work and her to stay home. My job traveled—99 percent of it was done via phone and internet, which meant I could do it from anywhere. Hers did not—it required lots of meetings, lots of face-to-face time, access to government terminals that existed only within the physical confines of a specific building.

Beyond that it was clear that I simply liked my job a whole lot more than she did, at the moment at least. So if we went out there, I would work.

We grappled with what that would mean for a typical workday. Well, she'd be home with the kids and I'd be there, too, ideally sequestered away in something like a home office. But I'd be there to help get the kids up. To help with meals. To take over when work was done and she'd had about as much of them as she could reasonably handle.

We tried to run a more thorough accounting of the numbers. We figured that relative to our current baseline, each month we'd be able to save . . .

- $3,000 in nanny wages
- $1,000 in reduced mortgage/rental costs
- $250 in train and metro fares
- $100 in gas
- $150 in workday meal costs

All told it added up to about $4,500 a month, which, while it didn't exactly account for the loss of all of Briana's after-tax income, sure made up a big chunk of it.

Plus, we'd be gaining time: fifty hours a week for her, and fifteen for me. We assumed that each of those hours had a dollar value equal to our respective hourly wages. When you added those up and factored in the decreased expenditures we came out way ahead in the ledger.

Eventually we talked ourselves into the view that it would be fiscally irresponsible of us to *not* move to Red Lake County.

In the end what it boiled down to for Bri was that she needed a break from her current job, and she didn't want to miss out on any more of the twins' childhood. Whether this was a long-term thing, whether she was abandoning her working mother identity to become a stay-at-home mom, whether this amounted to a betrayal or renunciation of all she had worked so hard for in high school and college? She didn't know. She would figure it out. What she did know was that this was what she needed *right now*, what felt right for her and for her sons.

I assured her, over and over, that she'd love the people in Red Lake Falls, that it was a totally different kind of community than the hardscrabble upstate New York towns we'd grown up in.

"Tell me about this Jason Brumwell guy then," she said. She saw a photo of him that had run in the story of my visit, all scruffy beard, dark glasses, and baseball cap. She wasn't impressed.

"He looks like . . ." she trailed off uncomfortably.

"A redneck?" I asked.

"A redneck."

"He's not a redneck."

"Honestly he looks a little scary."

"He's neither scary nor a redneck, and definitely not a scary redneck. He's a nice, sweet, thoughtful, educated guy. And everyone there is just like him."

"So they're all scary rednecks?"

It was a tough sell. The cold was another factor. I had to promise a lot—flannel sheets, warm mittens, a well-insulated house with a fireplace, if possible. "Remember, there's no such thing as bad weather!" I admonished glibly. "Only bad outerwear."

I knew, finally, that Briana was on board one day when I opened a package that had arrived in the mail and found two sets of Minnetonka slippers inside, one for each of the twins. "So wait, we're doing this? It's officially happening?" I asked.

"Yes, let's do it," she said. "But first go talk to your boss."

That, of course, was the remaining piece of the puzzle. All I had to do was convince *Post* brass that I should be able to stop showing up to work physically and instead live and file stories from a virtually unheard-of farming community 1,400 miles away from the action in the nation's capital. Easy!

In reality, it wasn't as crazy as it sounds. Newsrooms, perhaps more so than most other organizations, are ideally situated for remote work. At any given time the *Post* had perhaps dozens of correspondents filing stories from far-flung corners of the world and country. Some were traveling, some were based permanently in newsmaking regions like Silicon Valley and the Koreas, and some others had simply negotiated remote work arrangements upon hiring in order to stay in their current cities, chief among them New York. Telework, in other words, was already part of the fabric of the organization, and the *Post* already had the infrastructure—online meeting software, remote log-in capabilities, and the like—to handle it.

I was particularly fortunate in that my beat, such as it was, wasn't tied to any one exact place. If you're a Hill reporter, for instance, a big part of your job is wandering the halls of the Capitol and getting in-person quotes from policy makers. Being physically there is part of your job description.

My beat, on the other hand, was data. And in this day and age, data lives primarily on the internet, so that's where I spent most of my own time. Instead of roaming the halls of Congress, I spent my days digging through federal and academic websites looking for statistical diamonds in the rough—that's how I ended up with the ugly-counties story in the first place.

So in the middle of October I nervously scrawled some notes on a piece of paper and made the pitch to my editor: we'd move to Red Lake County in the following spring. I'd keep writing as I always did, via a home office that included a landline and high-speed internet access. Hell, I could even write periodic longer, data-driven feature-y pieces of interest to a national audience on life in rural America. I could come back to D.C. as needed.

We'd set a time period of a year, at which point we'd reassess: Were we desperate to come back to civilization? Was my work remaining consistent (or, ideally, improving)? Would we want to stay another year or move back?

And of course, we'd have an escape valve: if there was a sense that, God forbid, my work was getting worse as a result of being out of the office, I'd be willing to take any steps necessary to fix the situation—including uprooting everyone and heading back to D.C. for good, if needed.

My editor, Zach, was quiet throughout my whole spiel and when I was finally done he said, "Okay, sure, why don't you put together a memo and we'll run it up the flagpole and see what happens." There was neither pushback nor encouragement; the man reacted no differently than he would have if I'd asked for something completely routine, like an afternoon off for a dentist appointment.

But I wrote the memo and sent it to Zach, who sent it to his editor, who sent it to *his* editor, in a chain of editors reaching all the way up to executive editor Marty Baron, whose generally gruff no-bullshit demeanor can be summed up by the fact that the same actor who played

Marty in *Spotlight,* the 2015 Oscar winner about the *Boston Globe*'s efforts to uncover child abuse in the Catholic Church, also played Sabretooth in 2009's *X-Men Origins: Wolverine.*

"So basically Sabretooth decides whether we go to Minnesota?" Bri asked, when I mentioned how the proposal was being received at work.

"That's correct, yes."

A month later the official word came in—we were going to Minnesota.

Suddenly it was real. We sat down with the boys, then two and a half, to discuss what was happening.

"We're going to live in Minnesota," we said.

"Minnsota," they said. They had no idea what it meant, but the word soon became a universal totem of anticipation in the house, encompassing all our hopes, dreams, anxieties, our struggle for a better life. Minnesota.

One thing I figured I should do was let Jason and the other folks I'd met know we were coming. I didn't know exactly how to do this, though. "Hey, I called your community a shithole and then turned it into a circus for three days, and now I'm moving my entire family there!" What if it was an imposition? What if they were simply like, "What the hell is this guy on about?"

Eventually I shot Jason an email describing our plans. "I hope this doesn't seem too weird!" I wrote. "But the truth is I've thought about the place and everyone I met there a lot since my visit, and I think it would be a great place to live and raise the boys for a year or two.

And we're ready for a change—we've lived in plenty of places on the coasts, but never in the Midwest."

Then I waited for a response.

And waited.

And waited.

Five days later I still hadn't received a reply back. Jason had always been quick to reply in our correspondence leading up to and immediately following my visit, so I naturally assumed this was an ill omen. He had talked it over with some folks in town and was trying to figure out a way to tell me that no, maybe it might not be best for us to come out there. Or maybe it seemed like a completely weird, bizarre stalker thing to do. As Briana had wondered earlier, who the hell actually moves to northwest Minnesota?

Fortunately he put an end to my suffering later that evening with a characteristically chipper reply. "Wow Chris, this is unbelievable!" he wrote. He suggested we come out to visit and look at rentals and homes immediately. "We'd absolutely love to have you and whenever you plan your visit, plan on staying with us! I'll get some listings for area homes for you as soon as I can too!!!!" His exclamation points were reassuring.

Finding homes, as it turned out, was proving to be a challenge. We scoured realtor.com but there were never more than a small handful of places available in the area. Still, what we saw was promising: a five-bedroom house in Oklee for $45,000. A farmhouse with acreage for $100,000. With a D.C. salary, even on one income northwest Minnesota was our oyster.

Population density

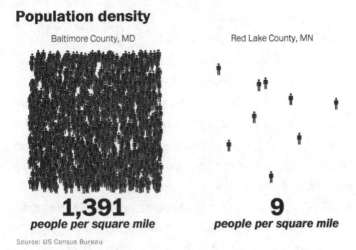

Baltimore County, MD

Red Lake County, MN

1,391
people per square mile

9
people per square mile

Source: US Census Bureau

Online, at least, there were no rentals to speak of. The closest Craigslist was for Grand Forks, North Dakota, and it listed zero rental houses for anywhere in or near Red Lake County. The papers, like the *Red Lake Falls Gazette* and the *Oklee Herald*, didn't have websites. It was looking increasingly like we'd actually have to buy something.

But as the months went on, even the promising listings started showing cracks. The $45,000 house in Oklee? A "fixer-upper" needing work. Same for the farmstead, on an even larger scale. Could we maybe camp in the barn while we fixed up the house? We were starting to find out why nobody ever moved to northwest Minnesota—it was impossible to find a place to live.

I started getting desperate, searching listings farther afield: Polk County, Pennington County, Duluth. It was all northern Minnesota, right? But Briana quickly put the kibosh on this. "You can't make a big stink about the 'worst place to live' in America and then move to the second- or third-worst place; that would be stupid," she said. She was right, of course. And capping my whirlwind romance with Red Lake County by moving my family next door to, say, Polk County would probably whip up an entirely new set of controversies. Best not to stir up any regional rivalries; I was already on thin ice.

Meanwhile, we started cluing in friends and coworkers to what we had planned. Reaction among other colleagues tended to be mixed, with a definite dividing line by age. Older coworkers, particularly ones with small kids, would come up to me and tell me how great an idea it sounded. "Wow, that's so cool!" is something I heard over and over again. "God I would love to get out of D.C." Clearly we weren't the only ones struggling with work-life questions.

Twenty-something coworkers, meanwhile, were curious but slightly horrified. "Do they even have internet out there?" a number of them asked. Yes, I explained. "What do people even . . . do out there?" Well, I said, I'm going to find out.

Briana faced a similarly divided reaction among her coworkers, particularly among the women. Some questioned whether she'd be okay walking away from a promising career that she was finally beginning to get established in. But others said yes, it'll be amazing for the kids and you can always come back to the career later when you're ready. Hearing that sentiment, particularly from some of the older women in the office, helped reinforce the idea that this didn't have to be a permanent change—she could come back. This was particularly true of jobs in the federal government, which has rules in place making it easier for people who've stepped away for a few years to return to work at their previous level of pay and responsibility, provided that a job is available.

My mom was ecstatic, a reaction driven primarily by her safety concerns. She fretted endlessly about the possibility of one of the twins tumbling down one of the three sets of steep stairs that linked our current living space together. The sidewalks around our place were dodgy and abruptly ended in odd locations, which combined with narrow twisting roadways meant that a grandson getting struck by a car was always in the back of her mind.

Briana's family was supportive, but a little more guarded in their response. Her parents, having lived the military lifestyle of frequent moves that took them far from family, understood that this kind of thing can happen in the course of a person's career. But a number of them asked, "If you're going to do that, why don't you just move back to New York to be closer with us?" We had, in fact, briefly considered this. But putting a few thousand miles between ourselves and upstate New York was a feature, not a bug, of our new plan. Our New York families were complicated, and all things considered it would be nice to have some distance between us and them.

As winter turned into spring I wrote to Jason and told him we'd like to take him up on his offer to stay if it was still open—it would be just Briana and me for a long weekend. We'd fly in to Minneapolis, rent a car, and drive up the state to Red Lake Falls. Bri would get to see some of the countryside that way, which she insisted on—keep in mind she had agreed to this whole adventure sight unseen, on the basis of my recommendation alone.

I mentioned we'd been having difficulty finding places, and Jason and his dad, Dick, got to work right away. They set us up with a Realtor friend of theirs and started asking around town to see who was privately selling a home, or would be considering doing so in the future. Dick and the Realtor, Loren, managed to rustle up a list of eleven properties to look at. Most of them had no internet footprint whatsoever—they were all but invisible to anyone looking for housing online. As we came to realize, private sales—direct transactions between a buyer and seller, unmediated by any Realtor or other professional—were a lot more common out there than in Baltimore.

On March 10 we arrived in Minneapolis and began our trek up the Minnesota countryside. Much of the Minnesota landscape, particularly in the eastern half of the state, resembles upstate New York—dense maple and pine forests covering rolling hills, dotted with small towns and lakes. Along the way we stopped at Lake Itasca State Park, where the mighty Mississippi River starts its journey from its source, just a tiny trickle a child can jump across.

We pulled over at a scenic overlook and turned off the car. The silence was profound, almost deafening. We hadn't heard anything like it in months, years maybe, so accustomed were we to the background din of a dense urban environment. After several minutes of adjustment our ears became attuned to a whole new soundscape, the subtle rhythms of nature that usually get buried beneath humanity's hue and cry—a rustle of leaves, a creak of ice on the lakeshore, an unseen animal skittering beneath the snowline.

The silence was a relief, and helped put our minds at ease about what we were getting ourselves into. Surely nothing but good could come of taking our children out of the clamor and bustle of the city to a quieter, slower place—one where they would have the space and silence to think, to develop an interior life, to learn to listen to and appreciate life's quieter, subtler rhythms.

Briana told me later that that moment at Itasca was a turning point in her decision that moving to Red Lake Falls was the right thing to do. "The silence . . . it filled me up," she said. "It was peace. I wanted our family to have that kind of peace."

We continued north and west, following the thinning forests to the plains. We got to Jason's house that evening, a little later than we thought we would. Dick came stomping down the driveway to meet us. "Well where in the hell have these east coasters been, who told us they'd be here at seven?" he thundered. Briana was mortified. Dick laughed a hearty laugh. "Welcome to Red Lake County," he said, offering her a big bear hug. "Nothing to worry about, you can't be any worse than that husband of yours."

We went in for a meal Jason cooked while Dick laid out the itinerary for our whirlwind real estate tour, which stretched out from one end of the county to another. "We've had people beating the bushes all over the place looking for somewhere for you to stay," he said. "You remember Chuck Simpson?" Commissioner Kiss-My-Butt. "He's been out there working harder than everyone; even he's excited you're coming to stay."

The next day started early. Most of the places we were scheduled to look at were for sale, not rent, but they were well under our price limit of $150,000. Dick and Jason drew what appeared to be a big distinction between places that were "in town" and those that were "in the country." Briana and I thought this was hilarious, since as far as we were concerned everything from here to Grand Forks was "the country."

But we soon understood that when folks in northwest Minnesota say "in the country," they mean it. One of the stops on our itinerary was a tidy little place on the edge of the county. To get there we drove through the fields of the western county on the paved roads, then turned off on a dirt road. No problem, we had lived on a dirt road for a period of time in Vermont. We could handle this.

After bumping down the road for a few miles we hitched a right onto an even smaller and more rustic dirt road. It appeared to be somebody's driveway but no, Jason assured me, it was a road. "I got the bus stuck at the turnaround up here a few years ago picking up the kids who live out here," he said.

After several bumpy miles we at last arrived at the property, a low-slung modular home on six acres. Aside from the house, a barn, and a shed there were no other buildings to be seen anywhere, in any direction. The nearest neighbor was miles away.

We toured the property and talked to the owners, Shari Rolf-Baird and her husband. "Yeah, it's pretty peaceful out here," Shari said. "Lotta space for the kids to run around; there's the whole barn for them to explore and build forts in." I could just picture it: Jack and Charles running about in the country, no cars, no strangers, no hassles. It was beautiful.

"Of course, you gotta keep an eye out for the wolves and the bears," Shari added nonchalantly.

"I'm sorry, what?" said Briana.

"We keep the rifle by the door for the wildlife, especially the bear. He's around so much we've got a name for him; we call him Brutus. Haven't had any problems with him yet but you never know."

After the tour we got back in Jason's car.

"No," Briana said before I had even opened my mouth.

"Come on," I said. "We can teach the kids about, like, wildlife safety."

"Absolutely not."

"But there's nobody around for mi—"

"That's exactly what I'm afraid of!" she said. "You think I want to be cooped up all alone in that house with you all winter? Me taking care of the twins and you trying to write and doing some kind of weird *Shining* thing? No."

"Okay, fair enough."

So that was "the country." We kept looking, visiting homes within the limits of the towns of Brooks and Red Lake Falls. We stopped for lunch in the middle of the day at Carol's Cozy, the only bar-restaurant in Brooks. When we walked in a bunch of workers from nearby farms were already in there, and it felt like a classic record-scratch, freeze-frame moment—conversation stopped, and all eyes turned to us as we walked in. I saw what I thought were a few familiar faces from my trip the previous summer, but they either didn't recognize me or didn't care to extend a greeting. Forget Minnesota Nice, it was downright Minnesota Nippy in there.

I began to feel a mild panic attack coming on. What the hell were we doing, anyway? Walking into a strange community a thousand miles from anywhere, assuming we could just set down roots and elbow our way into society? People usually move for familiar reasons—a job, a spouse, a family. According to the census, among people who moved five hundred miles or more in a given year, half moved for job-related reasons, a third moved for family, and about 18 percent moved for housing. Just 2.4 percent of long-range movers cited a reason that didn't fall neatly into one of those categories. But our move was 100 percent of our own volition, prompted by little more than a desire to get the hell out of D.C.

It was nearly inevitable that at some point I would write a story that would piss off a bunch of people in the country. Say, about gun control, or about the Republican Party. What would happen then? Would they show up at my door? Leave threatening messages on my phone?

I'd received plenty of angry and unhinged emails during my time at the *Post*, but nothing that ever made me fear for myself or my family. We lived in a large metro area where there was some safety, I felt, in anonymity. I came home from work and I wasn't Chris, the National Reporter, but Chris, the guy from 738 Pleasant Hill.

But that anonymity would be gone in Red Lake County—even if my relationship with the place hadn't been the subject of a media circus, there's no getting lost in the crowd in a small town. That's great for raising kids or feeling like a part of the community, but what happens if you do something that really pisses that community off?

Despite my misgivings, lunch went by uneventfully. At the end of it, in fact, the waitress surprised everyone in the place by bringing us all out a free slice of pie, on the house. Maybe I was overthinking things.

I didn't have high hopes for one of the last places we looked at, a property in Red Lake Falls that the Brumwells referred to as "the purple house." It wasn't much to look at from the outside—it was basically a large, light purple box with a garage attached. Given slightly different trim it would have been easy to mistake for an auto repair shop. But it was on a big lot, even by northern Minnesota standards, somewhere between a half and whole acre as best as I could tell. There were lilacs, lilies, and Concord grapes planted along much of the perimeter, although under the previous owners they hadn't been tended to for years. There was also the shadow of a huge garden near a spacious shed. If nothing else, there was lots of room for the boys to run around.

We went in through the garage and it looked like, well, a garage. No surprises there. I was prepared to write the whole place off until we stepped through the door to the house proper, where we were surprised to see a large, wide-open space with a gently vaulted ceiling. Everything had a fresh coat of paint. John and Sandy Klein, the neighbors who had purchased the place from the prior owners and cleaned it up to sell, assured us it was move-in ready—a big plus, given that we weren't going to have much time for any remodeling with a pair of two-year-olds in tow. Even more surprising, there was a spacious finished basement below, with three bedrooms in addition to the master bedroom on the main floor. One for the twins, one for guests, and one for my home office. Plus, a roomy play area where all the twins' toys and assorted toddler paraphernalia could go.

We tried to play it cool but I could tell by the look in Briana's eye that she was sold already—this was the place. Just thinking of what we'd do with it felt like winning the lottery. It had a staggering two and a half large bathrooms, more than either of us had had in a home in our entire lives. The two main bathrooms each had two sinks—one for each member of the family. I'd never lived in a place with a garage—this one had a double attached to the house. I'd also never lived in a place with more than a patch of a yard—this one practically came with a hayfield. The refrigerator even came with a built-in ice machine, an unthinkable extravagance. That comfortable, well-apportioned life—the one that seemed impossibly far away in D.C.—was now tantalizingly within reach.

We told the Kleins we'd get in touch with them and let them know the next day. But that night, over dinner at Jason's house, we resolved to put an offer in. The Brumwells, of course, got into motion right away to help us make it happen. Dick called on his Realtor friend Loren, who lived about an hour north, in the town of Grygla, to help us draw up the necessary paperwork. We inquired about a commission and Loren said he wouldn't hear of it; the house wasn't officially listed so he couldn't technically do anything with it anyway.

"Tell you what, get me a nice steak dinner after you get settled in town and we'll call it square," he said.

Late in the evening, when we were almost done with the paperwork, things hit a snag. Someone mentioned that there had been rumors of drug activity at the place before the Kleins had bought it.

"What was it?" Loren asked. "Were they manufacturing there?"

We had no idea.

"Because if it's a meth house," he said, "and there's chemicals soaked into the walls or the foundation or something like that, you might not know until six months after you move in and one of your kids starts having a seizure."

Holy shit.

This new information was paralyzing. I had done enough drug policy reporting to know that that assessment seemed extreme, but on the other hand I was no expert. How the hell would we get around this?

"Well, why don't we just give the sheriff a ring?" Jason said.

Briana and I were dumbstruck. "You can just do that?" we asked.

"Well sure, it's ten o'clock, Mitch is probably home right now," Jason said. "I've got his number right here on my phone."

Jason proceeded to give the number a ring and launched right into a chipper conversation, as if calling up the sheriff to inquire about meth houses was something he did every Saturday night.

"Yep. Okay. Thanks, Mitch!" he said, as he hung up. "Yeah no, there was no meth lab there," he told us. "They had some calls about possible drug use on the property, but they never heard anything about manufacturing on premises."

So there you had it. A question that could have derailed a home transaction for weeks in Baltimore County was resolved in Red Lake County with little more than a neighborly five-minute phone call on a Saturday night.

Early the next morning, paperwork in hand, we drove back over to the house to make an offer to the Kleins. John was a farmer and a trucker, gruff and a little intimidating with a horseshoe mustache, while Sandy was chipper and full of sunshine. We stood around the kitchen counter and hashed it out—within about five minutes we were all shaking hands over a deal. Dick and Jason were there, too, and though the topic hadn't even come up, Dick announced he'd put down the five-hundred-dollar honest money deposit. We objected, but we hadn't even thought to bring our checkbook. He had nothing of it. "Just send me a check whenever you get a chance," he said.

So that was it—later that day we were on our way back down to Minneapolis, purchase agreement in hand. We were going to be Minnesota home owners. It was starting to get real.

Over the next couple of months we packed up our life in Baltimore and prepared for the move as the Brumwells oversaw the home inspection and other technicalities in Red Lake Falls.

As May rolled up we finalized our packing and said our good-byes, and on the fourth we closed the door on our old house for the last time. We were going to Minnesota.

CHAPTER 3

Cross-country moves are generally a horrible affair and ours was no exception. I had the easy job, driving the rental truck stuffed with our belongings. Briana followed in our little Honda CRV, stuffed with Jack, Charles, Tiber (our seventy-pound beagle-basset mix), and Ivy (our twelve-year-old cat).

The CRV crew could only tolerate a few hours cooped up in the car before everyone started having meltdowns, so we stretched out the twenty-two-hour drive over five exhausting days. Technically, at this point, we still didn't even have a home to roll up to. We'd be getting in on a Sunday but the closing wasn't scheduled until the following day. But the Kleins told us they'd leave the door open and put the keys on the kitchen counter, letting us move in a day early. Not typically the way a real estate transaction would happen in Baltimore.

Eventually we pulled up to our new home in Red Lake Falls. The boys knew it by then only as the Purple House. We hadn't even gotten the kids out of their car seats before we were enthusiastically greeted by a sweaty, half-naked man. Rob Conwell, his name was, our new neighbor who lived across the street.

He was shirtless and sweaty because he'd been mowing his lawn, he explained. In about five minutes we'd heard half his life story—he was from Oregon, met a Minnesota girl who'd grown up in the area, they ended up moving back here to start a family two decades ago.

He and his wife, Alice, were active in music and theater in the area—did we play any instruments? There was a great little community band the next town over and they were always looking for new players; the conductor was fantastic and rehearsals were on Monday and Wednesday nights at 7 p.m. and—

"That sounds amazing," I cut him off, hopefully less rudely than it felt. "Maybe we can talk it over once we're all moved in?"

Of course, Rob said, of course. Welcome to the neighborhood!

We experienced a lot of this in the coming days and weeks—invitations to *get involved*. The Civic and Commerce Committee needed volunteers. The Northwest Minnesota Arts Council needed board members. The school needed a guest to come read to the kids. Churches needed folks to staff their basement dinners. Rural areas may not have a lot of people but they still needed to get stuff done. In the cities, economies of scale mean either these tasks are professionalized—people get paid to do them—or competition for the most desirable activities, like music and theater groups, is stiff. Here, by contrast, getting involved is easy. If you want to join a band or help with kids or put out fires, just show up. There's plenty of work that needs to get done.

As soon as we got the kids out of their car seats, Jack

tore ass up the garage stairs and into the house. Charlie, however, was transfixed for the moment by the garage. "Dad!" he screamed. "The Purple House has a garage door!"

The first order for the kids in the new place was to run around, opening and shutting all the doors and then flipping all the light switches they could reach. For the first several days you could always tell where in the house Charlie was by the "boi-oi-oi-oi-oing" of the spring door stops he was compelled to flick every time he entered a room.

"There's three bathrooms?" Jack said. *"That's crazy."* Indeed, compared to our old row house, where there was just one bathroom for all four of us, it was downright extravagant.

That first day the Brumwells and the Kleins came over to help us get all our stuff out of the van. Northern Minnesota boys don't fuck around when it comes to lifting and moving heavy things, and with their help we wrapped up the job in just a couple of hours—even though Ryan, Jason's brother, was deathly hungover from a wedding the night before. A few neighbors wandered over to pitch in as well, perhaps more out of curiosity than anything else. One of them, an old guy with a gray ponytail, brought over a six-pack and introduced himself as Larry Eukel.

Larry told us he had actually grown up on the property we now lived on, had swung on a tire swing from the very same oak tree that now overlooked the yard.

"It's a great place to grow up," he said, "and boy is it nice to see a young family in that yard again."

We subsequently came to learn that the property had something of a checkered past in more recent years. Neighbors told us of how, one summer, the electric company had shut off power to the place because the people living there hadn't been paying their electric bill. Well, the Presbyterian church sits right across the alley from the Purple House, and one morning staff arrived to find an extension cord running from one of their external outlets over to the garage. A handwritten note said it was connected to the freezer and could they please not unplug it? In the spirit of charity, they didn't. There were mean dogs in the yard, neighbors said. At one point somebody had parked an RV on the lot and appeared to be living out of it. Just a lot of weird stuff going on, and in a quiet, tiny midwestern neighborhood like this one, weird is bad.

The house is in an area of town known as the Hollow, a little quarter circle of the Clearwater River floodplain that's protected to the south and east by the modest hill leading up to the main level of the county. It bears the distinction of being the coldest neighborhood in town. One winter several years back, the Kleins told us, the water main under the street froze up and they were left without water until spring. The town told them to run a hose from a neighbor's house and they'd prorate both the bills. What else could they do? You can't unfreeze a northern Minnesota water main in February. I was glad Briana didn't learn about this until well after we had moved. And sure enough, our second winter here it happened again. The Kleins' water went dry, and they again had to run a hose to the other neighbor's place. Our water appeared to be fine but the folks at city hall instructed us to keep a tap running at all times, until the spring thaws came. They told us they'd just bill us our usual amount on our water bill so we didn't have to pay extra for the privilege of helping the town keep its infrastructure working.

Red Lake Falls feels like the kind of town your grandparents lived in, and I mean that in the best possible way. The town's 1,400 residents keep tidy homes on tidy lawns with sprawling vegetable gardens out back. To an adult living here for the first time, it feels like the kind of place you remember visiting during summers in childhood, where memories are built on lazy afternoons spent on broad, sunny lawns while the adults relax on a screened-in porch, cocktails in hand.

The town is home to a weekly newspaper, the *Red Lake Falls Gazette*, which publishes mostly high school sports news. In the summer when things get slow a new lawn gnome in someone's yard is enough to merit a front-page spread. While it's nice to see a small-town print newspaper alive, nobody would mistake the paper for a bastion of hard-hitting journalism. The contents are mostly taken up by photos of goings-on at the schools in town. Coverage of genuine local events, like city council meetings and the like, is virtually nonexistent. There was no coverage of local political races in 2016 and 2018, even though a dazzling array of candidates were on the ballot for everything from school board seats to county water commissioners. At one point the paper ran what appeared to be a story about a local college professor who gave his students a clever lesson illustrating the dangers of socialism. The story was fake, and had been cut-and-pasted from an email forward.

The town has two gas stations that double as social hubs—in the mornings different crews of cantankerous old-timers shuffle off to their favorite tables to discuss the day's news. There are two bars serving nearly identical foods and drinks at opposite ends of town, the kinds of laid-back midwestern places where little kids can be found running around in the back until late at night when their parents finally go home.

There's an independent grocery store, Brent's, that offers roughly the same variety of goods as the Grand Union in Oneonta, New York, did thirty years ago. Avocadoes are the most exotic produce they stock. For cheeses they have Swiss, cheddar, and something called "farmer's cheese," which is sort of like a milder version of Monterey Jack, if such a thing were possible. Transplants to the area inquiring about delicacies such as "goat cheese" or "cilantro" are met with quizzical stares. The meat section offers Norwegian delicacies like pickled herring in a jar and slabs of lutefisk around the holidays. There are large sections of the store devoted to pickling, canning, and sausage-making, with an underlying assumption that many locals grow or shoot much of their own food. Pet owners can purchase dried cat food at Brent's but not canned—the cats of Red

Lake Falls are evidently expected to do their own foraging as well.

There's a town library, which keeps a surprisingly liberal section of children's books in stock, including *Jacob's New Dress*, about a young boy who decides to wear a dress to school. Some controversy attended the addition of this book to the library in nearby Thief River Falls, where it was nearly banned, but parents in Red Lake Falls either didn't care or didn't notice.

There's a post office, of course, where you never have to offer your name or ID to pick up your mail because the employees already know who you are. There's the town pool, the one that residents fund-raised and built themselves, where Alice, the head lifeguard and our neighbor, will encourage your children to strap on a life preserver and take a plunge off the diving board even if they haven't fully mastered how to swim yet.

The town's four houses of worship encompass its religious diversity: one Catholic, one Presbyterian, and two flavors of Lutheranism. The pastor at Bethany Lutheran, Gary Graff, made a point to stop by our house, welcome us to town, and invite us to attend worship there if we were so inclined. There are two small doctor's offices offering limited standard services like checkups and X-rays several days a week.

There's a small pharmacy, open nine to five Monday through Friday, where the staffers inquire about your ailments with genuine concern, and will gladly tell you all about theirs if you've got a minute to stop and chat.

There is industry in town—Homark, a manufacturer of modular homes, and Wood Master, a maker of outdoor wood furnaces. A paved trail runs from the golf course at one end of town to the farmland at the other, following the length of the old railroad bed and traversing the Clearwater and Red Lake Rivers via sturdy steel trestle bridges.

Those first few days were a whirlwind of new faces—smiling ones, much to my relief. People from all over town dropped off welcome baskets—baked goods, fresh produce from gardens, a surprising variety of pickled vegetable products. Beth Solheim, an older woman with roots in the town who now lived several hours away, stopped by to drop off a watercolor portrait of Tiber that she had painted, based on a photo she'd seen of him on Facebook.

After a decade in the city it's a shock to move to a place and realize that everybody already knows who you are. People we'd never met would stop us on the street and ask how we were liking it so far, diving into deep personal conversations as if we were familiar friends who'd just had lunch together a few days ago.

One day not long after we moved in we got a call on our new landline phone, which we had to put in since the cell reception was spotty to nonexistent. Briana answered; it was a receptionist at one of the doctor's offices. This was odd because we hadn't been to the doctor's yet.

"Hey, are you guys home?" the receptionist asked, casually.

"Umm, yeah, why?" Bri asked.

"Well, the UPS guy is here and he says he tried to drop off a package at your place but nobody was home, but I told him I was pretty sure you were there today. Do you want me to send him back down there?"

"Uhh, sure, thanks?" Bri replied.

After a while we started to get used to our notoriety. Part of it was due to the publicity that had attended our decision to move, sure. But eventually we realized that this was simply the kind of place where everybody knows everyone—and they even know whether or not you're home.

A few weeks after the move we attended the wedding of Heather Wallace, Jason's sister. The reception and dinner were held at the American Legion on Main Street, which we thought was weird—did we have to be veterans to get in? But no, out here the Legion posts were basically just public bars, where anyone could walk in and grab a drink. Inside, dusty old photographs of previous Legion luminaries with strange Scandinavian names lined the wood-paneled walls. The wedding was closed-bar, but the Legion beer was cheap. For dinner there was an enormous vat of pulled pork, a staple at large gatherings in the area. Jack and Charles mingled with a crowd of kids of all ages at the back of the hall, where the door was propped open and children ran freely in and out well into the wee hours of the warm early summer night.

The sense of community contrasted sharply with what we had previously experienced in places like Vermont and Maryland. One of our neighbors in our old row house, we'll call him James, kept mostly to himself, for instance. He was a strange guy, a little older than me, and didn't work because he was on disability due to an ankle problem, or so he told us.

Since he didn't have a job he was always around, and he could be prickly toward his neighbors. Shortly after we moved into our home there he blew his top because, in mowing our tiny patch of a lawn, we had mowed a little bit over onto his portion of the grassy hillside. Weird guy, in short, and we generally tried to avoid him (bad neighbors connected by a common wall: another drawback of high-density living).

One day early in the summer before the twins were born we noticed that James's car had been parked outside his place for several days but nobody had heard or seen him around. This was strange because we'd usually see him coming or going, or hear him or his TV through the walls, often at late hours of the night. But for several days now, silence.

After a week went by we spoke to some of the other neighbors on our row of six houses. No, they hadn't seen him, either. It was odd, of course, but none of us were what you'd call his friends, and nobody wanted to try to dig deeper and risk getting involved with whatever weirdness he was surely involved with.

As we learned later, James's mother, who lived across town, had been trying to get in touch with him, too. No luck. Roughly two weeks after we had noticed him missing, she came by his house with flowers. It was his birthday.

She knocked on the door; no answer. She tried the handle; it was locked. Windows were locked, too. The house was all sealed up. Not knowing what else to do she called a locksmith and the police. They forced their way in and followed the smell to where his body lay alone in the basement, dead by his own hand. He had killed himself two weeks ago and nobody had any inkling.

We felt a little bit of guilt—was there anything we could have done? But of course, there wasn't. We didn't know the guy, our interactions with him tended to go poorly, and if we were being honest, life became a little easier knowing we wouldn't have to hear him banging on the walls at 3 a.m. or screaming at us because of a lawn-mowing impropriety. James's tale became a macabre story we told acquaintances and friends. Bri was about six months pregnant with twins around this time; one of our close friends remarked that during the two weeks his body lay in the basement, James's ghost had traversed the wall between our units and taken residence within one of the twins. We all laughed. But that's life in a lot of cities—surrounded by humanity, you can still die alone.

Needless to say, when I tell this story to folks in Red Lake Falls they gasp in shock and disbelief.

The thing I remember most from those first few weeks is the collective sense of wonder at having a home—a real, honest-to-goodness single-family home. I had grown up in one of these, after all, so it represented something of my default expectation for what a family should live in. But after a decade on the pricey east coast it had seemed like the expectations of childhood were being trampled by the cold fiscal realities of metro life in the twenty-first century. Out here, though, it was different.

Perhaps our greatest sense of having "made it" as adults came one evening shortly after our move. The kids were in bed and we were watching TV on the couch. At the show's end I got up to go to the bathroom, prompting Briana to leap off the couch and run into the room ahead of me, a trick we often played on each other in Maryland.

"Come on, you've gotta be kidding me," I said. "I really have to go!"

"You realize we have two other bathrooms now, right?" she asked before shutting the door in my face. I was thunderstruck. It was a revelation—no more fighting over the one cramped little commode of our Maryland house. If we both had to take a dump at the same time we could do so, in private and at our own pace, like civilized people. It seemed extravagant. According to the U.S. Census's Survey of Construction, in 2016 just 3.7 percent of new homes were built with one bathroom or less, while about 35 percent had at least three or more. Moving from Maryland to Minnesota vaulted us from the bottom 4 percent of the American toilet distribution almost all the way to the top third.

The house seemed huge to us. After we'd lugged all our belongings in—everything that had our old place bursting at the seams—there was still empty space everywhere. We turned some of the leftover space downstairs into a play area for the twins. In the coming weeks Briana filled it with maps and educational posters, as well as the twins' collection of toys brought from Maryland. It was like having a preschool classroom right in the house. The twins were thrilled to have a space of their own to ransack and make a mess of, as they saw fit, provided they cleaned it up somewhat before bedtime.

The house isn't huge by any stretch of the imagination—maybe 2,000 square feet, roughly 25 percent smaller than the typically newly constructed home, according to census figures—but to us it may as well have been a palace.

We started to understand the profound effect of living space one evening after dinner, when Jack and

Median home listing price

Washington, DC   Red Lake County, MN

$493
per square foot

$53
per square foot

Source: realtor.com

Charles linked arms and announced they were headed off to the playroom together to play. They were typically fractious; they often quarreled and squabbled over toys and attention and countless perceived slights, real and imagined. But after years of constant policing and keeping a watchful eye on their every move, suddenly here, in Red Lake Falls, in a house with space they could truly call their own, for the first time they were ready to go off and be themselves by themselves, with no need for parental intervention. They finally had the space to become themselves without constantly chafing against each other. If tall fences make good neighbors, large playrooms make good siblings.

People with an affinity for dense urban spaces— many who happen to be employed at the universities and media outlets that shape so much of contemporary public opinion—tend to take a dim view of the classic single-family home. They take up too much space. They foster car culture. They're unsustainable from an environmental standpoint. High-density housing—condos and apartments—is far preferable to suburban sprawl, or so they tell us. It's better for *everyone*.

But a lot of the writing on this topic doesn't really grapple with the draw of the single-family home to begin with, the huge place it occupies in the American psyche and culture. For a body of thought that deals with the proper role and uses of physical space in society, it's remarkably blind to the importance of space to individuals. It doesn't wrestle with what it can really mean to a person to not have to share walls and floors with noisy neighbors. It doesn't fully appreciate the difference between living out one's life in a cramped space versus an expansive one. To have ample outdoor space to run, to breathe in, to call your own. The market urbanists in the nation's media centers acknowledge, on some level, that people tend to desire these things. But many of the people who write about the topic don't seem to truly understand these desires themselves. That's a big blind spot, especially considering that so many of these people are responsible for creating the culture consumed by the entire country.

Beyond that, the market urbanists seem to view the choice of living spaces as a binary one: either you're in the cities (high density, good) or the suburbs (low density, bad). Given that roughly 80 percent of the country lives in the cities or their suburbs this is an understandable place to start the discussion, but it overlooks the completely different modes of living available in small towns and rural areas.

Then there was our new lawn. Given the sheer size of it—approaching three-fourths of an acre—it was clear we'd have to get a proper lawn mower to take care of it, something I'd never had to do before—we'd relied on a small human-powered reel mower to deal with our tiny patch of Maryland greenery.

I picked up a proper gas-powered push mower from Wal-Mart that spring and was excited to give it a spin for the first time. But the instruction book said I needed to add some oil to the engine before I fired it up, and damned if I couldn't figure out how to get the oil cap off.

The cap was an odd-looking yellow thing. I twisted it, pulled at it, tugged it this way and that. It didn't budge. I referred to the instructions. I pulled up YouTube videos on my phone. Nothing.

Miraculously, after I'd been puzzling over the mower for about an hour a pickup truck pulled into the driveway. It was Michael Baker, the fire chief in the nearby town of Plummer and an engine mechanic at Arctic Cat in Thief River. He'd been one of the local voices gently chiding me on Twitter after my first story ran, sending me photos of the view of the Red Lake River from his back porch.

"Gonna do some mowin', eh?" he asked.

"Only if I can figure out this oil cap," I said. He walked over, crouched down, and popped the cap off with a flick of his wrist.

"Here you go," he said. I thanked him and finally got to mowing. As of this writing, more than two years after that day, I still haven't changed the oil on that mower. The truth is I still can't figure out how to get that cap off.

At the *Post* I'd penned a number of columns railing against lawns. "Lawns are a soul-crushing timesuck and most of us would be better off without them," I wrote on August 4, 2015, less than two weeks before I saw the words "Red Lake County" for the first time. They soak up water—nine billion gallons *a day* nationwide, according to the U.S. Environmental Protection Agency—they kill native biodiversity, and according to the American Time Use Survey the average American spends more than seventy hours a year on lawn and garden care. What a waste!

I still believe all this on some level. And yet that summer, when I stopped to consider *my own lawn*—my own patch of land, an environment for me to shape and cultivate as I pleased, a place for my children to play, grow, explore, and run free—I couldn't wait to get out there and start mowing for myself. One of the foundational principles of statistics is that what's true at the population level is often not true at the individual level. The average American can expect to live 78.6 years— but that doesn't mean that *you*, the individual reading this book, will live that long. Maybe you'll live to be a hundred. Maybe you'll get hit by a bus tomorrow. Who knows? The point is, things can be true for populations that aren't true at all for individuals. Do I still believe the median American lawn is a waste of space? I do. Would I defend my own to the death, weed whacker in hand? Absolutely. The numbers often make hypocrites of us all.

Lawn care in northern Minnesota is a highly fraught topic, filled with land mines for unsuspecting newcomers. People here trim their grass down to about the length you'd find on a putting green. If your grass is much higher than that you're expected to apologize for it to everyone you meet, especially if someone catches you outside doing something other than mowing it. You're responsible for upkeep of the sidewalk in front of your house, too, which includes keeping weeds from growing in the cracks. One day that summer I was outside with the boys and Rob, the half-naked neighbor, came by. He gestured toward a couple of dandelions springing from a gap in the sidewalk. "Growing a hedge, eh?" he said. He didn't need to say anything else. After the boys were down for a nap I slunk back out to the sidewalk with the weed whacker.

One of the first things we wanted to do after moving in was to start a garden. There was already space on the property set aside for that, a partially fenced-in corner of the yard that had been used as a garden in years past but which was now just a tangle of weeds and long grass.

We spent several weekends cleaning out the light brush and mending the fence all around the garden plot—we'd see regular patrols of deer in the neighborhood in the evenings, and rabbits were everywhere. Plus, Dick Brumwell showed us a picture of a black bear that he'd been watching rummage through his bird feeder that spring. We didn't know what bears do to gardens and didn't want to find out.

Finally, it was time to work the soil. The garden area was too large to till by hand, but the Kleins had a large, gas-powered roto-tiller from the farm they let us borrow. One thing we came to understand was that pretty much everyone up here owns "equipment."

One mild Saturday afternoon I finally took the tiller to the garden. It was satisfying work, guiding the machine along a gridded path, turning dead grass and compacted dirt into rich, fluffy black soil. At one point when I was nearly finished I took a break and turned the tiller off, and that's when I heard the sounds.

They were tiny, almost imperceptible squeaks. Kind of like little birds, but the pitch was a little off. I searched for the source and found it coming from the ground, one of the patches I had just finished tilling. I shoved some dirt aside, and realized with shock and horror that I had roto-tilled a nest full of baby rabbits.

They were tiny, with their eyes barely open. They had been grievously wounded by the blades of the tiller, but unfortunately none of them was quite dead.

Shit.

When I was a kid, about eleven years old, a group of my friends and I came upon a baby bird on a sidewalk that had fallen out of its nest. It had no feathers yet and its eyes weren't open. It was very badly injured and appeared to be gasping for air. We knew we'd have to put it out of its misery, and after a few minutes of hushed discussion it was decided that one of us would ride over its head with our bike tire, which was the most humane option for ending its suffering among the limited tools we had at our disposal. As the son of a veterinarian I was elected to carry out the mercy killing. I rolled my tire forward and there was a quick crunch and then it was over. To this today I have occasional agonizing dreams involving small, delicate creatures past the point of mending and in horrible pain.

The rabbits were the bird all over again. It was obvious that they were beyond repair—taking them to the local veterinarian was out of the question. But I couldn't simply leave them there to suffer in the dirt until they expired. Instead I opted for the humane choice—I walked into the shed and grabbed a metal shovel. I used it to decapitate each of the wounded rabbits as swiftly as I could. The work was excruciating, but mercifully short. I placed the tiny bodies in a bag for the garbage and worked the blood-soaked dirt back into the bed of soil with my boot. Thus was the Ingraham family's Minnesota garden consecrated.

I had kind of a queasy, uneasy feeling afterward, like a nightmare had come to life. But part of me was strangely invigorated. After all, wasn't this part of what we came out here for? To get out of the city and closer to the land, to live a life where the stakes were real and messy, where we'd be exposed to nature's teeth and nails and learn whether we had any of our own?

Granted, killing five baby rabbits with a shovel didn't exactly make me Grizzly Adams. But it made me a little different than the person I'd been back in Maryland. When I told coworkers and friends from the east coast about the rabbits, they recoiled in shock and horror: "Oh, the poor bunnies!" they'd say. When I told folks in Red Lake Falls about the mishap, on the other hand, it barely merited a reaction. "Eh. Gotta do that sometimes," John Klein told me.

Several weeks later another baby rabbit appeared in our garage one morning. It was older than the ones I'd killed in the garden, old enough to be out hopping about on its own but not smart enough to avoid getting stuck in the garage. I saw an opportunity for redemption.

"We talked about getting a pet rabbit when we came out here, right?" I said to Bri, holding forth the baby rabbit in a cardboard box. "Maybe this is a sign. This is how we atone for the dead bunnies in the garden."

"You realize wild rabbits die pretty much immediately when you try to bring them into a house, right?" she said. "They freak out. They literally die of fright. Their hearts basically explode."

"Not this rabbit," I said. "You watch. This rabbit is here for a reason. It has a purpose. This rabbit will live."

It was dead by the next morning. Another tiny corpse wrapped in a grocery bag and set in the trash.

After that we decided the only thing to do was to purchase some proper domesticated rabbits. We picked a pair up at a nearby county fair later that summer. We bought them off a kid who was charging ten bucks apiece, cash, for them. We gave him a twenty and he handed us a box with two rabbits inside. Easy-peasy. The kids christened them Mubba and Bubba, since "mubba" had been Charlie's word for rabbit when he was still learning how to talk.

Among our other animal adventures that first summer was a memorable trip with the kids to Carl Schindler's dairy farm. This was the same place I visited during my reporting trip, where I proved my regular guyness by letting a calf suck on my hand. Now it was the twins' turn.

Carl took us all to the main barn so the boys could feed the cows some hay. He showed us how to pick out the tightly packed leafy bits of the hay that the cows really liked. The boys were a little put off by being surrounded by a herd of thousand-pound beasts with big wet noses and long, rough tongues, but they took to it surprisingly well.

As we petted the cows, I saw out of the corner of my eye the mangy old yellow farm dog from my prior visit trotting up to us. His tail was wagging and his head was high. He had something in his mouth. When he got a little closer I realized it was a dead kitten.

Charles turned and examined the gruesome spectacle. "Kitty sleeping!" he said.

"Ha-ha, yeah, kitty . . . sleeping," I said.

"Oh geez, sorry," Carl said. He shooed the dog out of the barn. "Been a while since he did that," he said nonchalantly.

"Kids, we're not in Baltimore anymore," I said.

"Kitty sleeping," Jack said.

That first summer we spent many of our evenings and days down at Voyageur's View, the Brumwells' campground and tubing business. The place had kind of a perpetual spring break vibe—on the weekends in particular big groups of college-age kids would rent out campgrounds and spend the days drinking on the river and the nights drinking by the fire. Large groups would often come down from Canada—the border was only ninety minutes away. Those groups had a particular reputation for rowdiness. Canadian kids evidently treated Red Lake Falls the same way American kids treated, say, Tijuana—a place to drink and go wild south of the border.

But as many people in town explained, when the Brumwell siblings took over the business from their dad, Dick, they actually cleaned things up a lot—requiring advance reservations to camp and cutting down on after-dark partying, among other things—in an effort to put a more family-friendly face on the business. It seemed that everyone in town under a certain age had worked at the campground as a teen one summer or another, and they all had hair-raising stories to tell—drunken brawls, knife fights, late-night debauchery of all sorts. Ryan and Jason had spent nearly all their childhood summers at the campground and partook in the madness from a young age, drinking and partying with friends and campers starting in their early teens.

Those days were over, however. They had spent enough beer-soaked nights at the campground for many lifetimes and now, as adults taking over the business, they wanted to dial things back. Folks in town generally gave them credit for their efforts, even if there was still work to be done.

One of the twins' favorite things to do at the campground was ride around in the short red bus the Brumwells used to deliver firewood to the various campsites. They'd clamber into the back, where the seats were stripped out and replaced with a wobbly pile of firewood rising up to the ceiling, and then hold on for dear life as Ryan or Jason or whoever tore ass around the property, stopping to drop off wood and shoot the shit with their often drunk clientele.

Briana and I were mortified the first time they did this—is there anything more dangerous than letting a two-year-old bang around on top of an unsecured wood pile in the back of a bus rattling down a bumpy dirt road? But the Brumwells seemed unfazed by it, as if it were something they did every day. Eventually their ease became ours.

The campground was an education for all of us that summer. The boys got to ride around the place on all manner of recreational vehicles the Brumwells had lying about—golf carts and ATVs and beat-up old buses. Going fast, off-road, atop a vehicle powered by a combustion engine was simply part of the fabric of childhood out here. For the boys' third birthdays Briana and I had got them tricycles. I had dreams of teaching them the simple pleasures of being outdoors on a bicycle. But the Brumwells one-upped us by getting them Power Wheels, the little battery-operated vehicles that kids sit on and operate with the push of a button. I was trying to teach them the joys of human-powered transit, but the Brumwells were giving them an education in how kids in rural Minnesota got around.

The nights at the campground tended to go late. One of the most disorienting things we experienced after the move was the length of the late spring and early summer days in northern Minnesota, on account of how far north we were. Red Lake Falls is farther north than the northernmost tip of Maine. It's farther north than Toronto, Montreal, and Quebec City in Canada. In fact, it's farther north than more than half the entire population of Canada, owing to how much of the Canadian population is packed into the southernmost section of the country that dips down into the Great Lakes. Demographically speaking, it's accurate to say that Red Lake Falls is farther north than Canada.

The extreme latitude means that summer days run long. On the solstice the sun doesn't set until 9:30 p.m., a full hour later than in D.C. But the sky remains light far longer than that, owing to the tilt of the planet. True darkness doesn't arrive until well after midnight, and the sky begins to lighten again less than ninety minutes later. D.C., on the other hand, gets more than five hours of total darkness on the summer solstice.

The long evenings mean that the neighborhood kids are often out late on summer nights. The playground at the park down the road didn't really start to get hopping until about eight o'clock at night. One evening one of Melissa Benoit's sons, four-year-old Henry, rang the doorbell to see if Jack and Charles wanted to play. It was quarter after nine.

That playground was something else to get used to. It was made of wood and steel and dated back at least to the time the Brumwell boys were small children, and maybe even earlier. It was huge, towering at least three times the height of the more safety-oriented play structures the twins knew from Maryland. The slides were fast and the modern safety features, like rubberized surfaces and rounded corners, were virtually nonexistent. It was the kind of place where a kid could really break a femur. Naturally, the twins loved it.

One thing we couldn't get over about the neighborhood kids was how nice they were. Even the older kids would welcome Jack and Charlie into their games that summer. Without any prompting they'd help the little ones clamber up a difficult playground ladder, or loosen the rules of whatever games they were playing to accommodate the clumsy toddlers.

Briana and I had never seen anything quite like it. When I was a kid, for instance, if a younger child attempted to horn in on whatever game we were playing we'd tell them to fuck off, in exactly those words. Here, however, the kids were kind, warm, welcoming to little strangers. You could tell that they enjoyed it, too—they weren't taking Jack and Charlie under their wings simply because adults expected them to.

One day we saw a group of older kids, maybe twelve or thirteen years old, hanging out by one section of the playground. One of them was holding what appeared to be a packet of cigarettes, and they were all discussing it heatedly. They had clearly found it in the park and were trying to decide what to do with it. In upstate New York in the early 1990s there would have been no question: we'd take those cigarettes off to a secluded corner of the woods and then we'd smoke them.

Imagine my surprise, then, when the kid holding the smokes eventually broke off from the group and walked over to the garbage can near Briana and me and tossed them in. "We found these in the park," the kid said. "And we didn't want the little kids to pick them up so we're throwing them out."

"That . . . is absolutely the correct thing to do?" I said, dumbfounded. Was this some kind of weird trick they were playing? Like some kind of knockout game variant where they were gonna crack me over the head with a rock and then put it up on Snapchat? But no, they tossed the cigarettes away and then went back to whatever it was they had been doing before.

"Did that really just happen?" I asked Briana.

"That really just happened." Rates of teen smoking have fallen by roughly 75 percent since the two of us were in high school, so perhaps we shouldn't have been so surprised.

These Minnesota kids are okay, I thought. We might actually make it here.

CHAPTER 4

The transition from commuting to D.C. to working from home was, so far, everything I could have hoped for. We would get up early with the boys, get them fed and dressed, and then I'd head down to the office, coffee in hand, to fire up Twitter and catch up on whatever fresh horrors the 2016 campaign was dishing up on that particular day.

Things were proving to be more challenging for Briana, however. She had the hardest of our two jobs: managing the children all day long. She would take them on hikes at a local nature preserve or go on a day trip to see the headwaters of the Mississippi on Lake Itasca, ninety minutes away. But whatever the drawbacks of working for the federal government, there was no question that her new bosses, at three years old, were proving much more difficult to manage than her old ones.

Our new life was, in some ways, a double whammy: she was feeling both the acute isolation of being cooped up at home with small children all day, and the loss of the many close friendships she had forged in Maryland. Unlike me, she thrives on human contact. She missed her "tribe"—friends, coworkers, fellow moms—back in Ellicott City.

Briana and I are, strictly speaking, high school sweethearts. We met the summer after my senior and her junior year of high school, interns at a biological research station on Otsego Lake in Cooperstown, New York.

Briana and I sparked a friendship, then a romance, over tubs of seaweed and cultures of fecal bacteria in the lab. I went off to college at Cornell University and a year later she followed. We dated through most of college, with a few breakups thrown in for good measure. And we married not too long afterward, when I was just twenty-four and she twenty-three.

From a big-picture economic standpoint our upbringings hadn't been too different—if the Ingrahams were middle-middle class for upstate New York in the 1990s, the Wilsons were lower-middle. She was one of four children in a very religious military family. In the course of her childhood her dad had been stationed in Pennsylvania, Georgia, Germany, and Arizona, so she had moved around a lot. After her dad retired from the military when she was ten, they moved to the tiny town of Jordanville in upstate New York to be closer to family roots.

Their first night in Jordanville the family stayed in a camper on the property where their new home was being built. It was nearly finished and would be move-in ready in a day or two. That night the family was awoken by the sound of shattering glass. Briana's dad jumped out of the camper and ran toward the house, where he found several young men in the midst of trashing the place—smashing windows, kicking in cabinets and doors, tearing fixtures off the walls. The men fled to a pickup truck and drove off. In the course of speaking with the police and other people in the community they found out that a rumor had been started that Briana's mother was black. Somebody had paid a group of yokels twenty bucks to trash the house and send a message that "that's not okay around here." Briana's entire family is white but it didn't matter. In upstate New York in 1991, the mere rumor that a black person was coming to town was enough to prod the good old boys into action. Briana's dad got the plate number of the escape vehicle and gave it to the police. The police told him that the truck owner denied he was involved and that there wasn't anything else they could do about it. The racially motivated violence would go unpunished and uninvestigated. Welcome to New York.

For most of her childhood her family was just barely holding on to the bottom rung of the middle class. They were fiercely proud of the fact that they never had to rely on food stamps, and looked down on those who did with a ferocity that only people who've barely missed the cutoff for government assistance will understand.

Briana's mom wanted her to be a nun, but by the time she was in her teens Briana had gotten other ideas in her head. She was the only one of her siblings to fully throw herself into her studies at school, driven in part by her Catholic-girl fear of letting down the adults in her life. But even at a young age, she knew she wanted a better future for herself than what her parents were able to provide. A foundational moment in her childhood happened at the age of twelve, when she stumbled upon her mom's bank statement and saw that the balance was negative. "How could a family have less than zero?" she asked herself. At that moment the precariousness of her parents' financial situation became apparent to her, and as she tells it she vowed to herself, that day, that she would do whatever it took to ensure that as an adult, there was never a negative balance on her own bank statement.

She excelled at school—she was involved in sports. Art. Singing. Theater. She didn't just join academic clubs, she became the president of them. With that drive came opportunities from completely outside the family orbit—an Outward Bound trip to Maine, environmental camp in the Catskills, a congressional youth leadership summit in D.C., a summer scientific excursion to Puerto Rico. Since her parents couldn't pitch in to cover family costs, Bri saved up the money herself from the jobs she worked after school, and researched and applied for all sorts of scholarships and grant programs to help make the trips a reality.

Those trips had opened her eyes to the possibilities of the world that lay far beyond the borders of Jordanville, and by the age of seventeen she had come to see the small town as a dead end and couldn't wait to go off to a four-year college—the first in her family to do so. We met that summer, when she was headed into her senior year and I was already off to Cornell. In the throes of a summer romance she decided to apply there, too, and unlike myself (the beneficiary of legacy admission preferences, thanks to my dad) she qualified for admission solely on the basis of her own talent and drive. She was one of just a handful of students in her graduating high school class of eighteen kids to attend a four-year school, and it was an Ivy League one at that.

From the minute she set foot in Ithaca, New York, the town of Jordanville represented the past, a place of limited viewpoints and few opportunities. It would always be her childhood home, with all the attendant messiness and complication, but it stood in opposition to the bigger, brighter, more exciting world beyond.

She dove into her studies at Cornell with the same enthusiasm she'd shown in high school, managing a double major, a double minor, and a year abroad in Geneva, Switzerland, some theater and singing for extracurriculars, all while also working constantly at two, sometimes three jobs to support herself (her parents had made it clear from day one that any educational expenses were hers alone to bear).

From Cornell we traveled together to Southern California for an ill-fated year at the University of California, Irvine. I was enrolled in an English PhD program, primarily because I dreaded the idea of entering the workforce and wanted to prolong the lax academic lifestyle for as long as possible. She was working on a master's in history.

That year I essentially crashed and burned; having lived in bucolic corners of upstate New York my entire life, the suburban madness of Orange County was simply too much to bear. I stopped going to class and spent my days mountain biking, the landscape (or what was

Where Briana and I have lived together

left of it) being the area's one redeeming feature. Briana, having bounced all over the place as a child, was more adaptable. She didn't much care for the place, its materialism, its politics, its utter unaffordability. But she didn't mind it as much as I did, either. It was just another place, after all, like Pennsylvania or Arizona or Germany.

I ended the year with two "did not completes" and an F on my aborted graduate school transcript. Briana, on the other hand, had managed to accelerate her coursework and escape with her master's degree a full year early, despite the additional burden of a thirty-hour-a-week waitressing job to help pay the bills. At the end of the academic year we fled to Vermont, and then several years later Briana's government job brought us to Baltimore, where she went to work for the Social Security Administration.

She excelled at her job, rising up rapidly through the

ranks on the basis of her talent and her enthusiasm for the work. She solved thorny policy problems in the disability arena, helping spearhead an initiative that drastically reduced the waiting times for federal disability assistance for people with the most intractable medical conditions.

There were headaches, of course, but the work provided a deep sense of meaning—she could confidently say that she was helping people, that the world was made a better place by her actions. Plus, the job was the ticket to the solid middle-class security that life at her parents' house had lacked. It had become a big part of who she was.

Now, in Minnesota, that part of her identity had been stripped away. It's a shock to go from days filled with meetings and high-stakes policy decisions to the fulltime care of two small children. You start to forget what it's like to be a professional adult. The person that you are slowly gets replaced by the person your kids need you to be. Every parent goes through this on some level, but Briana experienced this transition in its most extreme form.

We talked a lot about it those first few months, after the kids went to bed. Or rather, she did—I'm a crappy conversationalist but a half-decent listener. It wasn't that she regretted the move, exactly, but it was a big change for her in a way that it wasn't for me. I still had a job, coworkers, obligations to the wider world. She no longer had any of those things. I tried to tell her things to put the situation in the best light. Think of all the time we have now, I'd say. All the things you get to experience with the kids that you missed before. Think of the incredible privilege we have to be in this situation.

The privilege, of course, was all mine, and she reminded me of that. There's nothing privileged about chasing three-year-olds around all day. Nothing privileged about being thousands of miles away from your dearest friends. Nothing privileged about giving up a career that you worked decades toward.

There were good moments in those first few months, magical ones even. But there was no doubt she was in a funk. It was proving more difficult than I'd expected, too. One thing that we, as a society, don't fully acknowledge is just how difficult, how taxing, how utterly exhausting and draining it is to care for little children. It is *work*, in the purest, rawest sense of the word. And in early childhood, a time of screaming and fighting and boundary-pushing and frustration and potty training and neediness, above all the endless, incessant neediness, the rewards can be few and far between. I would get off work and go straight into the living room to relieve Briana from twin duty. There were many days when I missed that long commute, the hours of peace and quiet on the train. The twins were just so much.

I began to doubt whether we'd make it here. The strain it was all putting on her made me nervous. Maybe she was heading toward a meltdown like the one I'd had in Southern California, where I couldn't take it anymore, just had to get out, as far away as possible. I had made us abandon SoCal, so it would only be proper and fitting for us to leave Minnesota for her sake.

But Briana, as I should have known, is a much stronger person than I am.

We started by putting the kids in day care a day or two a week, with Jason Brumwell's sister, Heather. It felt like a weird thing to do at first—wasn't the whole point of coming out here to get the kids *out* of day care? But Briana needed it, and hell, I needed it, too. The extra time freed her up to respond to one of the probably dozens of volunteer opportunities that people had dangled in front of us since we got here.

She started with the Zehlians, a local chapter of the General Federation of Women's Clubs. It's a service club, and they put her to work doing everything from teaching art history to fourth graders to delivering meals on wheels. Then she joined the board of the Northwest Minnesota Arts Council, a nonprofit funding arts projects in the region. Then a local chorus. Then the University of Minnesota, Crookston Concert Band, which happened to be short on oboe players. At the urging of Dick Brumwell, she rounded up some local business leaders to restart the Red Lake Falls Civic and Commerce Committee.

Soon she was being invited by various civic groups all around the region to deliver talks about our experience moving out here. I had been doing this as well, until the *Post* put the kibosh on it—scrutiny on the media is tighter than ever these days, and my bosses didn't want to give the impression that their reporter was in the pocket of the Northwest Minnesota Soybean Growers' Association.

After one of these events, Briana overheard a pair of women talking in the lobby.

"I saw her husband give a talk about their move, too," one of them said. "Honestly hers was a lot better."

But that remark encapsulates a lot of Briana's experience of moving out here. When we first got here, it irked her somewhat to be known primarily as "that reporter's wife." Now, more often than not, people in the area know *me* as "Briana Ingraham's husband." My identity basically hasn't changed since coming out here—I'm still the *Washington Post* reporter. But she's had to rebuild hers from the ground up: first as a mother, then as a volunteer, and now as a pillar of her community—a phrase I'm able to say, for the first time in my life, without the slightest hint of irony. Because there's a true *community* out here, in a way that there wasn't in upstate New York, or in Vermont, or in Maryland. And a community like this one needs people like Briana—people who thrive on making things better. It's not a difference that you'd necessarily even notice if you were just driving through a place like Red Lake Falls. You have to live here for a while to understand it, have to feel how people like Briana, and the Brumwells, and Al Buse are the lifeblood of a small town.

CHAPTER 5

This is going to sound strange to anyone who hasn't spent much time in the Midwest, but the prairie is a lot like the ocean. It's broad and vast and flat and has a way of making you feel tiny, insignificant, but in a good way. The texture of the landscape is also constantly changing: black soil sprouting tiny shoots in the spring, growing to a green riot in the summer and then turning to shades of gold and brown in the autumn, and then finally, as winter approaches, returning to black as the last remnants of the harvest are plowed back under to await the spring.

In the summer you can sit by a field and watch the wind blow its designs on the tassels of the corn, as mesmerizing as a rolling sea. It's hard to learn to appreciate these things from the window of a car going eighty miles an hour down a highway, which is how most of us experience farm country (if at all). But as our first summer in Red Lake Falls went on we were learning to watch and listen to the land. The boys acquired an odd taste for dried soybeans and the freshly hulled wheat kernels that a friend who worked at the local grain elevator had dropped off in a bucket—"wheat crunchies," they called them. One day in late summer as we drove out of town on some errand or another I pointed out to the boys a lumbering green machine ambling through the fields. "Check out that tractor," I said.

"No, it's a combine," Charles said matter-of-factly.

Exactly one year, to the day, after I had penned the initial story that eventually brought us to Red Lake Falls, I sat in a dunk tank in the parking lot of the American Legion, on Main Street, as part of a fund-raiser for the town pool.

Being in a dunk tank is one of the few occasions a grown-up can hurl invective at elementary school kids in public without fear of censure, and I took full advantage as kids stepped up and lobbed softballs in my direction. But the finest arms of J. A. Hughes Elementary School were out in force that day and they were hungry for revenge—I was dunked into the lukewarm tank, mercilessly, over and over as kids squealed in delight, a fitting vengeance for the journalistic malfeasance I had inflicted upon the unsuspecting town.

Red Lake Falls isn't a wealthy community by any stretch. But when there's a call for help people respond. That day in August, for instance, the town of 1,400 people managed to pull together $70,000 to fund some needed maintenance on the town pool—the equivalent of $52 for every single man, woman, and child in the community.

Service and volunteerism—the forces that keep many rural Minnesota towns afloat—happen to be the same things Briana thrives on. Economists and demographers have a name for this—social capital. "The links, shared values and understandings in society that enable individuals and groups to trust each other and so work together," as the Organisation for Economic Co-operation and Development puts it. Many places in America are suffering from a social capital deficit, most famously outlined by sociologist Robert Putnam in his book *Bowling Alone*. Americans are withdrawing from one another, Putnam's argument goes. Social trust is declining, neighbors are becoming strangers to one another, political divisions are putting up walls between people. Instead of joining a league to bowl with others, we're increasingly just bowling by ourselves—if we get out of our houses and away from our screens at all.

One way sociologists indirectly measure social capital is via census response rates. People who take the time and effort to diligently fill out their census questionnaires every ten years are, the thinking goes, more likely to be civically and socially engaged in their communities. They understand or intuit that an accurate census count is necessary for a representative government to function properly.

As it turns out, the upper Midwest has the nation's highest rates of census response. Red Lake County's response rate of over 86 percent puts it in the top tier of counties nationwide on that measure. By contrast, the median U.S. county's response rate is 81 percent. Some of the lowest rates of response are found in places like Alabama, where in one county fewer than half of residents filled out their census forms in 2010.

You don't even need to trust the spreadsheet on this one: spend a little bit of time in a place like Red Lake

County and it's impossible not to notice that people here are highly invested in their community. See that little park with the gazebo on Main Street? Dick Brumwell built it as a memorial to his late wife, Diane. See that garden on the hill across the street from the county courthouse? That's a project of the local Lion's Club. See that train-shaped light display on the old railroad trestle during the holidays? That's the brainchild of Jim Benoit, who thought people should have something nice to look at when they drive into town.

Social capital is built, in part, on trust. Americans, in general, have grown more wary of their neighbors over the years. Data from the General Social Survey, a long-running survey of American attitudes, show that the share of Americans saying most people can be trusted has fallen from nearly 50 percent in the 1970s to just over 30 percent today. A 2014 YouGov survey found that more than three-quarters of Americans said they keep their doors locked when they are at home.

In Red Lake Falls, on the other hand, I haven't met anyone who locks their doors when they're at home. Many rarely even lock their doors when they're not home. People here trust each other so much that they often leave their cars running with the keys in the ignition when they run into Brent's to pick up some groceries. Neighborhood kids, as I've mentioned, often run about unsupervised well into the evening hours—not a problem when you trust the folks in your neighborhood to keep an eye out for any trouble. And of course there was the time Dick Brumwell wrote us a five-hundred-dollar earnest-money check for the house we eventually bought, despite his having known us for approximately thirty-six hours.

Crime in Red Lake Falls is virtually nonexistent—mostly bad checks and the occasional drunk driver, if the weekly sheriff's report in the *Gazette* is to be believed. The latest county-level federal crime data for Red Lake County, from 2014, show that that year there were 0 murders, 0 rapes, 0 armed robberies, 1 aggravated assault, and 13 reported instances of property crime in the county. That works out to a violent crime rate of about 25 cases per 100,000, or one-fifteenth of the national average.

In 2018 I got summoned to serve on jury duty at the county courthouse. It was essentially a three-month, on-call deal: I had to be ready to show up for any cases that came to trial in a three-month period. To my disappointment, none did.

Trust and social capital are so high in Red Lake County in part because it's so demographically homogeneous. A number of researchers, including Robert Putnam, have noted with some dismay that diversity tends to erode social capital. Americans simply tend to trust people more when those people look like them. Red Lake County, if you'll recall, is 93 percent white. It's one of the whitest counties in the country. The biggest demographic schism is between Catholics and Lutherans.

I've thought a lot about this during our time here. Would the people of Red Lake Falls have been so welcoming if I were, say, a black reporter? And what about me—would I have moved my family halfway across the country if the ugliest county had turned out to be, say, a majority-Hispanic county along the Mexican border?

I wish I could answer an unequivocal yes to both those questions but the truth is I don't know. Social scientists know that all of us are subject to beliefs and attitudes that are motivated by racial attitudes we barely understand or are even aware of. The technical term for this is "implicit bias," which is really just a polite way of saying "racism."

What I can say definitively is that, as a white guy, I see a lot less casual racism tossed around in Red Lake County than I've seen in upstate New York. Not long after the twins were born, for instance, Briana and I visited a bar in the town of Little Falls, New York, near her parents' home. At the end of the night we stopped on our way out and struck up a drunken conversation with an older couple who were standing outside having a smoke. Somehow the topic of kids came up and we mentioned we had twins.

"Oh, good," the man said. "Be sure to raise them white."

"Raise them right?" Briana asked. We thought we had misheard.

"Raise them *white*," he said, poking the air with his cigarette for emphasis.

We didn't need to ask what that meant. "White" was code for "one of us," an upstanding citizen, a full person, a member of the in-group. Nonwhite would be, well, everything else—everything wrong with the world.

Imagine what kind of environment you have to live in—what kind of people you have to surround yourself with, the types of things you have to believe and discuss with them on a regular basis—that telling strangers to raise their kids white is a just a normal utterance that pops out in the course of a casual conversation. How saturated with racist ideology does a community have to be before "raise them white" passes almost for a greeting between strangers on the street?

Briana exploded with rage before I even fully registered the comment. "What the FUCK?" she yelled, stepping up close to them. "Who says that? WHAT THE FUCK IS WRONG WITH YOU?"

I had known her for about fifteen years at this point and had never seen her like this. I had to physically pull her away from the situation, dragging her toward the car as she screamed profanities at the couple. My only thought was avoiding a brawl with drunk racists outside a Little Falls dive bar at 1 a.m. on a Saturday.

That's upstate New York, where a lot of people assume that it's safe to say racist things if you're talking to another white person. You're on the "same team," after all.

In conservative, rural northwest Minnesota, by contrast, I've never observed even the slightest inkling of these things. I don't assume it's some magical realm where racism doesn't exist—Minnesota folks are subject to prejudices just like anyone else. But any racism here isn't the type that openly speaks its name to fellow white strangers on the street.

Research, incidentally, backs this up. In 2015 an economist named Seth Stephens-Davidowitz compiled reams of Google search data on variants of the n-word. He controlled for usage that wasn't as likely to be linked to prejudicial attitudes—for instance, appearances of the word in the context of hip-hop lyrics.

That study found that the highest percentage of racist Google searches occurred along much of the Appalachians, extended well into upstate New York and parts of New England. Certain pockets of the South, unsurprisingly, were also hotbeds of search engine racism.

Nearly every region of the study west of the Mississippi, by contrast, had much lower than average instances of racist Google searches. That includes nearly all of Minnesota, with the exception of the northeastern region of the state.

Again, this doesn't mean that those regions have liberated themselves from racism. It only means that the prejudices at work in those parts of the country aren't the type that you type directly into your Web browser, looking for racist jokes, perhaps, or for like-minded people to subject to a rant.

Jack and Charlie's godparents happen to be black, close friends of ours from Maryland. Kelly, the twins' godmother, worked with Briana at Social Security. "How are you gonna expose those boys to different cultures when you're living all the way up there?" Kelly asked us once.

It was a good question. How do you raise children to

appreciate everything the world has to offer when you live hours from the nearest "real" city? Would we be depriving them of the rich cultural experiences that cities and more diverse areas provide by raising them in Minnesota? Kelly and her husband, Sean, have come out to visit us a couple of times now. They had their concerns, initially. During Kelly's first visit here, for instance, she had been worried about driving while black in northwest Minnesota. She didn't have any issues, fortunately, not then and not during any of the other trips she's taken out here to visit. But as a black motorist visiting an area that's roughly 95 percent white, it's the kind of thing that never really leaves your mind.

After several trips out here, experiencing the place, meeting the Brumwells and some of the other folks in the area, Kelly and Sean feel a little more at ease about their godsons' upbringing. Sean grew up in a tiny little community in Virginia, just a few thousand people. So he understands the draw of the small-town life, even if it's not what he chose for his own kids. But they still do little things to make sure the boys don't lose touch with their Baltimore roots. They made the boys an "essential black music" Amazon playlist, for instance—Prince, Stevie Wonder, Al Green, the classics. For Christmas in 2018 Kelly and Sean got the boys a book called *K Is for Kwanzaa*. I'm reasonably certain they're the only six-year-olds in northern Minnesota who know what a dashiki is.

On the other hand, there is culture of a sort up here—plenty of it, in fact. Norwegian festivals abound in the summer, where you can eat lefse, learn about Scandinavian history, and watch re-creations of famous Viking battles. There's a rich agricultural tradition in the area, memorialized in places like the Tri River Pioneer Museum in Plummer, the Engelstad Pioneer Village in Thief River Falls, and the annual Western Minnesota Steam Threshers' Reunion in the town of Rollag.

Every fall L'Association des Français du Nord, a local nonprofit, hosts a French-Canadian festival in the largely forgotten town of Huot, in eastern Red Lake County. The festival draws French-Canadian musicians and artists, as well as members of the Métis Nation—a primarily Canadian community of mixed Native American and Anglo-French heritage.

There is culture and diversity here, in other words; it's just the type that you have to actively make an effort to seek out and experience. It's not like living in a big diverse city, where you can experience the world simply by walking down the street.

We did, however, find Minnesota culture to be sorely lacking in at least one respect: the food. Minnesotans have forged deep attachments to their culinary traditions over the years, which is unfortunate because Minnesota food is almost universally bad. Minnesotans are particularly fond of "hot dish," which is a folksy midwestern term for what normal people refer to as casserole.

Minnesotans wax rhapsodic about their hot dish, particularly to newcomers. This is puzzling—during my childhood, casserole was typically something my mom made when she was too busy to cook a proper meal.

Casserole was always something to be served with an apology. In my experience there's little to distinguish Minnesota hot dish from casseroles served elsewhere. It typically consists of a mishmash of spare ingredients held together with a glue of cream of mushroom soup.

Minnesotans are particularly fond of "tater tot hot dish," which is basically a casserole in which one of the ingredients is frozen, pre-made tater tots. It tastes about as good as it sounds, although Minnesotans consider it the ne plus ultra of upper midwestern cuisine.

Hot dish is probably held in such high regard in part because Minnesotans have very little in the way of real cuisine to compare it to. The dominant culinary tradition in the state is Norwegian, and if you aren't familiar with Norwegian food it's probably because there's very little reason to eat it outside of Norway. The most famous Norwegian dish in Minnesota is lutefisk, which is freeze-dried cod reconstituted to a gelatinous texture and baked in an oven. It's exactly as appealing as it sounds.

Minnesota's lutefisk tradition is largely kept alive in community suppers held in the basements of Lutheran churches around the holidays. Nobody in Minnesota actually *likes* lutefisk, but they hold on to the tradition partly out of spite (if I had to eat this as a kid, the thinking goes, then I'm going to subject my own kids to it as well), and partly because when it comes to food there simply isn't a whole lot else to cling to.

The counterpart to lutefisk is lefse, which is a bland flatbread whose primary appeal is that it isn't lutefisk.

Lefse is *okay*. It's a perfectly serviceable product for human beings to ingest. If you were a member of an advanced alien civilization raising a large number of humans as pets, you'd probably feed them lefse for the same reason that alfalfa pellets are fed to captive rabbits: it provides adequate nutrition and is not likely to upset anyone's stomach. Lefse is what a food scientist would invent if she were tasked with creating a less exciting alternative to white bread. Lefse is fine.

There's also walleye, of course, a favorite of anglers that Minnesotans rave about despite it being a perfectly unremarkable type of whitefish. Like lefse, walleye benefits from the comparison with lutefisk. Minnesotans love walleye; it's the state fish and the Department of Natural Resources keeps strict quotas on the number that anglers are allowed to catch and keep in a season. Walleye is the lefse of fish: bland and inoffensive, and cherished by Minnesotans simply because it's here.

Minnesotans view intense flavors with suspicion. The driving principle behind Minnesota cuisine is blandness: if in doubt, add water, flour, or mayonnaise. Minnesotans display a quiet sense of pride at taking their coffee black, for instance, but this is only because what passes for coffee here would be charitably described as coffee-flavored water elsewhere.

In 1984 the Minnesota legislature designated an official state beverage: milk.

Minnesota pizza is universally bad. Shortly after we moved we ordered a takeout pizza from one of the local bars and were shocked to discover it was topped, among other things, with cheddar and American cheese. Last summer I was hanging out at the Brumwells' campground when one of the campers brought over a homemade pizza to share with the staff. It was topped, no joke, with sliced grapes. I screamed.

The best pizza in Minnesota is DiGiornio's. The second-best is Domino's. Eating any other pizza is not advised.

On another occasion we went out to try the food at the closest Mexican restaurant, which was twenty miles away, in Crookston. The fare was not noticeably different from what the median Minnesotan might be expected to concoct from an off-brand supermarket Mexican meal kit: the tacos, for instance, were topped with iceberg lettuce and shredded cheddar cheese. Perhaps they got this idea from the very popular "taco in a bag" found in hot trucks here. It's literally a bag of Doritos, with lettuce, tomatoes, and sour cream added on top.

Another product you won't find in northwest Minnesota: any type of sparkling wine drier than grape soda. Ask for "champagne" and you're likely to be served a Moscato that tastes like carbonated corn syrup. Try to order a "Prosecco" and you'll be asked to speak English, please. One benefit of a small town, though, is that you can typically wheedle storekeepers into carrying stuff you want, especially if you buy a lot of it. That's how Bri and I solved our Prosecco problem—once we explained what it was to Mike Swendra, titular owner of Mike's Bottle Shop, he was happy to keep some of it in stock for us. Judging by our monthly alcohol bill, I suspect it was a wise business move.

The sad truth is that northwest Minnesota may be one of the most culinarily impoverished regions of the nation. One thing I expected northwest Minnesota to excel at, given the popularity of hunting here, was venison. I was sorely mistaken. There is no rich tradition of venison steaks or venison rib or venison soups in this part of the country. No, the common thing to do with venison up here is to grind it up, adulterate it with large amounts of ground pork, and turn it into sausage. It's nominally referred to as "venison sausage," but you'd have a hard time distinguishing it from a typical store-bought sausage. This is partly on account of the pork adulteration, and also due to the fact that northwest Minnesota deer feast on soybeans and corn all throughout the autumn. The mild diet removes nearly all trace of gaminess from the meat, which, from the standpoint of the typical Minnesotan's taste buds, is just fine.

Adding to our own particular misery was the fact that we were saddled with two three-year-olds who were picky eaters even under optimal circumstances. Minnesota cuisine is, in fact, perfectly calibrated toward the diet of a three-year-old who refuses to eat anything other than chicken nuggets and french fries. As a result I've given up all hope of my children becoming adventurous eaters. Several weeks ago one of the twins tried a slice of Domino's pizza and complained that it was "too spicy."

Minnesotans are, however, the unacknowledged masters of one culinary realm: pickling. This is in part a reflection of their heritage: in Scandinavian countries, as in Minnesota, the growing season is short and people rely heavily on canning and pickling to make summer's flavors last through the winter.

You can't buy real Minnesota pickled products in stores—the best pickles come directly from neighbors and friends, by the jar and bucket toward the end of summer. Our first summer here, Jim Benoit, a retiree living on the south end of town, stopped by one day with a plastic ice cream tub filled to the brim with pickles from his garden. Inside, cucumber slices soaked in a broth of vinegar, onions, garlic, and what appeared to be entire dill plants. Each bite combined salt, tartness, and crunch in perfect proportion.

We found other ways around the region's food short-comings. Amazon turned out to be a lifesaver—not just for "exotic" food items, like curry paste, but also for staples that we otherwise would have had to drive long distances for: diapers. Wipes. Dog food. Cat litter.

Amazon helped ease the transition from Maryland, where we were no more than twenty minutes from a store selling literally anything we needed, to Red Lake Falls, where the nearest Home Depot's an hour away and specialty retailers are virtually nonexistent. Judging by the questions we got from some Marylanders about our move, a fair amount of city folks' reservations about moving to the country involves difficulties of buying stuff you might currently take for granted, like clothing or toys or housewares. That might have been the case thirty years ago—moving to the country might have entailed a certain type of material deprivation for the well-heeled—but Amazon and the internet in general render those concerns more or less moot.

There were notable exceptions, however. In December 2018, for instance, we decided to add a bearded dragon lizard to the family zoo. Beardies, as they're known, grow to about two feet in length, most of which is tail. One of them can be comfortably housed in a fifty-five-gallon aquarium. Their heads, necks, and the sides of their bodies are covered in rubbery spikes, which give them a misleadingly fierce appearance. They have a reputation for being outgoing and curious, and don't mind being picked up and handled the way many other reptiles do. Ours, whom we named Holly, gets particularly snuggly as she's falling asleep, and will gladly nuzzle against a warm human hand or neck or chest for comfort.

One of the first things we discovered about Holly was that she likes to eat. A lot. And the thing she loved the most when we first got her was crickets. From the get-go, I knew that keeping an ample supply of crickets on hand would require some planning. The closest pet shop, the PetSmart where we purchased her, is an hour away in Grand Forks. Restocking our cricket supply would require a time commitment of at least two hours out and back.

By Christmas Day that year, Holly's cricket supply was running low. I decided to order crickets online, a first for me, in order to save the trip to North Dakota. I bought the crickets from Fluker Farms in Louisiana, one of the more well-established online insect vendors. There are, in fact, hundreds, perhaps thousands of websites that will ship a dazzling array of live insects directly to your home—crickets and mealworms, sure, but also more exotic fare like hornworms, silkworms, black soldier fly larvae (for example, maggots), waxworms, millipedes, roaches. But as a neophyte I opted to keep things simple: 250 crickets, which seemed like a reasonable amount for a lizard who was theoretically capable of gobbling up to fifty of them every day.

I sprang for the next-day shipping to ensure there was no gap in Holly's cricket supply. But the package ended up getting delayed by a fierce blizzard that roared through the northern plains that week, dumping up to a foot of snow and sending temperatures plunging below zero. The cricket box ended up spending an unplanned overnight at a FedEx sorting facility in Grand Forks. I feared they would all be dead on arrival.

On Friday morning I anxiously met the FedEx delivery man at the door. He appeared to be relieved to unburden himself of the six-inch-square box emblazoned with the words "Live Insects" and decorated with life-size cricket silhouettes. We exchanged no words. If you're a FedEx driver, you probably try to avoid conversations with the types of people who order boxes full of insects from the internet.

Having never ordered internet crickets before, I naively assumed that I'd open up the box and find the crickets in some sort of sealed bag or plastic bin to facilitate easy transfer to their final storage place in the home. I also assumed that given the near-zero temperatures we were experiencing that morning, any crickets in the box would be groggy and disoriented and easy to manage.

I was wrong on both counts.

I cut open the tape and opened the cardboard flaps and was greeted by dozens of beady little cricket eyes staring eagerly up at me. I had a brief vision of the aliens in the claw machine from *Toy Story* before the crickets started doing what they usually do when they are suddenly exposed to light—hopping maniacally. I quickly closed the flaps before too many escaped.

This was a conundrum. There was no immediate way for me to transfer 250 clearly active and ravenously hungry crickets from the box to the shallow plastic container we were storing them in at home. The only solution would be to grab a spare fish tank we had out in the shed (incidentally, the one we had briefly kept the doomed stray bunny in), which would take a bit of time, requiring a trip outside in the deep snow and chilling cold. Back at my desk, after all, I had a nearly finished story that was due to my editor. Rather than upend my workday for the sake of $11.50 worth of internet crickets, I decided to retape the box and store it in a secure location until I had time to deal with it.

In retrospect, this was a huge mistake.

Given the disruptive possibilities posed by the dog, the cat, and the twins, there was only one place where I thought I could put the cricket box without it getting overturned or split open: the bathroom adjacent to our kitchen. I put the crickets in the cabinet above the toilet and went back to work. For about twenty minutes, everything was quiet.

Just as I was about to file my story, I heard Briana, in the kitchen, utter the following words: "Where are all these goddamn crickets coming from?" I should point out here that I told her offhandedly that I had bought crickets online, but I hadn't told her when they'd arrive and she hadn't been around when FedEx came.

At this point, I reasoned that there was no crisis, that she had probably encountered one or two stray crickets that had hopped out when I initially opened the box. So I decided to keep working.

As I was making final edits to the story, I continued to hear increasingly frantic cricket-related outbursts from the kitchen. Briana later told me that she first realized something was terribly wrong when one of the cats suddenly leaped onto a pumpkin pie that had been warming on the countertop. It was going after an unusually large cricket that was munching the filling.

Eventually the commotion was too much to ignore. I went to the kitchen. Briana whipped around to face me, wild-eyed.

"So uh, remember when I said I ordered some crickets?" I said. "They got here toda—"

"*Yes, I see the crickets are here,*" she said. "*Why are they all over the kitchen?*"

"Huh," I said. "That is weird. Let me check something." I walked over to the bathroom. I opened the door.

There were crickets. Everywhere.

Crickets on the floor. Crickets on the walls. Crickets in the sink. Crickets in the toilet. A clump of at least twelve crickets were attempting to cram themselves underneath the baseboard. A cricket jumped at me from the stack of folded washcloths on the shelf. Two crickets appeared to be chasing each other around the plunger. The crickets in the toilet were propelling themselves around the bowl at an astonishing speed.

For some reason my first instinct was to flush the toilet, as if that would do anything to solve the problem of crickets in all the other places that were *not* the toilet. I shut the door. "Uh, don't come in here!" I yelled. My voice was unnaturally high from trying to force myself to sound nonchalant and cheerful.

Evidently, I had not resealed the box as well as I should have. Later inspection also revealed that in my haste to ascertain the crickets' condition, I had opened the box from the wrong side, despite the presence of large arrows indicating the proper side with an all-caps warning that read,

SEE INSIDE FLAP FOR CARE INSTRUCTIONS!

There was nothing to do now but execute the Spare Fish Tank Protocol on an emergency basis. I threw on my boots, ran out to the shed, and grabbed the spare tank. I brought it back to the bathroom, threw the box inside it, and began scooping up the strays wherever I could find them.

Roughly forty-five minutes later, the bathroom was clear. But in the interim, the earlier escapees had begun migrating elsewhere. There were crickets in the kitchen closet. Crickets in a pile of shoes. Crickets making their way downstairs to the kids' playroom. The cats were in a state of high alert, having what I can only imagine was the greatest day of their lives.

I tried to collect all of them. It was like the world's shittiest game of Pokémon. Well after the initial cleanup concluded, crickets kept turning up in inconvenient locations throughout the day. They were in the playroom and under the couch. At one point I heard Charles shout gleefully from the bathroom, "There's another cricket in the toilet!"

We did, eventually, round up all or nearly all of them, although I imagine there's still a contingent of them lurking in the kitchen closet to this day. Several days afterward, Briana approached me in the kitchen with a grave look on her face.

"The crickets made me realize something about you," she said.

"Uh-oh," I said.

"It's always been crickets in the bathroom with you. Always."

"I . . . don't follow?"

"It's the way you do things. You *try* to do the right thing, but you just . . . don't try enough." She opened a kitchen cupboard, where I had jammed all the Tupperware in a chaotic jumble. "Crickets in the bathroom," she said. She pointed near the door, where I had taken

Beardie ownership, by the bug

Holly's total bug consumption in her first 60 days

🦗🦗🦗🦗🦗🦗🦗🦗🦗🦗 **500** crickets

🪱🪱🪱🪱🪱🪱🪱🪱🪱🪱 **500** mealworms

🪳🪳🪳🪳🪳🪳🪳 **350** dubia roaches

🪱🪱🪱🪱 **200** black soldier fly larvae

🪱 **50** superworms

off my wet snow pants, jacket, and mittens and left them on the floor. "Crickets in the bathroom." She walked me to our bedroom closet, where I had placed a pile of dirty laundry on the door of the laundry chute, but hadn't bothered to actually open the door and toss the clothes all the way down. "Crickets in the bathroom." She walked me back to the living room. "Charles, come here," she said. Charles ambled over.

"Who dressed you today, Charles?" she asked.

"Daddy!"

She turned to me. "What color are his socks?"

I looked. One dark red with astronauts, the other dark blue with dinosaurs. "Well, at least they're both—"

"Crickets in the bathroom," she said.

I didn't expect the bearded dragon to prompt a profound shift in how we understood the dynamics of our marriage, but here we were.

After the great cricket escape, I switched to a live dragon food that was slower-moving, not prone to jumping, incapable of climbing slick surfaces, and not prone to chirping in the middle of the night. In mid-January the FedEx guy brought the first shipment, of many, of these wondrous new bugs. I brought the box in, placed it on the kitchen table, and opened it up.

"Aha!" I said. "See, these come in a plastic container *inside* the box! No risk of escape!"

"What are they?" Briana asked, coming over for a closer look.

"Roaches!" I popped off the top, revealing dozens of brown, scuttling creatures in a pulsating mass.

She looked me dead in the eye, turned around, and walked out of the room without saying a word.

To think that, had we still been back in Maryland, with a Petco right up the road, none of this would have happened.

As of this writing we are still married.

CHAPTER 6

But I'm getting ahead of myself now. Back to that first summer. One of the visitors to our home was a poofy long-haired orange cat. It showed up in the yard one day, got chased up a tree by Tiber, and yowled until I came over to rescue it. It followed me around for the rest of the day, and subsequently started coming over to visit every day.

The cat was extremely friendly and appeared to be fairly healthy, so it was evidently being cared for by someone. But nobody in the neighborhood seemed to know who. Jason Brumwell remarked that it had often sat at the bus stop with the kids in the mornings during the school year. Melissa Benoit said it had gotten itself into their basement one summer and was stuck there for an unknown length of time. When she finally freed it, it stuck around, so Melissa offered the cat some food, which it ate ravenously.

The cat started sleeping at our house: it had to be shooed out of the garage in the evenings, and we'd find it curled up on the rocking chair on the porch first thing in the mornings. We started feeding it. One afternoon when a particularly fierce thunderstorm rolled through town, accompanied by a tornado siren, we made sure to scoop it up from outside and bring it downstairs to the basement to huddle with the children, our pets, and us as we waited for the all-clear. From that day forth it assumed it had the right to enter the house whenever it pleased, and started pawing at the window of my office and yowling whenever it saw me in there.

Whether we liked it or not, the cat appeared to be adopting us as its owners. We called it Orange Cat, because everyone in the neighborhood just referred to it as "the orange cat." Orange Cat was shockingly gregarious, and unlike our skittish gray cat Ivy, who had always been terrified of the twins, Orange Cat would let them pet her and didn't flinch whenever they came trundling over shouting "kitty!" at the top of their lungs. I also hold certain beliefs about orange cats vis-à-vis cats of different colors, stemming from my childhood: we had a fat orange cat named Butterscotch who had a bobtail and was the best cat any boy could hope for. He wasn't shy, he loved to play, he sought out the company of people. While I do not have any hard evidence to back this up, I firmly believe that orange cats possess certain genetic traits that make them cooler and generally more bad-ass than other cats. Nearly every veterinary clinic I've been to, for instance, has a clinic cat that just loafs about the place and generally gives zero fucks about anything: those cats, in my experience, are almost always orange cats. When we lived in Vermont, our neighbors had an enormous orange cat named "Compton" for his general street smarts and devil-may-care attitude. Garfield? Orange cat. Morris, of Nine Lives fame? Orange cat. Captain

Marvel's Goose? Orange cat. Winston Churchill had an orange cat, named Jock, he loved so much that after his death, his family insisted that an orange cat be kept at Chartwell, his estate, in perpetuity.

We developed an understanding with our own Orange Cat: we would provide her food and shelter in the garage, as needed, and in return she would make herself available for pets and chin scritches to all members of the Ingraham household. She happened to be a ferocious hunter, and as a deal sweetener she took to leaving decapitated bats and choice mouse organs for us on the porch.

Everything was fine up until the day I got a text message from Heather Wallace, one of Jason's sisters: "Trouble on Facebook, you better take a look."

Indeed there was. Heather had attached a screen shot of a neighbor's Facebook status, someone I realized I still hadn't met. "Love it the new people that wrote a bad review on red lake falls moved next door to me," the guy wrote. "Today he come into my yard and steels [*sic*] my plums off my tree wow and I have never meet [*sic*] him some balls."

Wait, what?

"Not to mention feeds and houses our cat, that she no longer comes home," a woman, who appeared to be his wife, wrote in reply.

"Go tell him to quit feeding her," a friend of theirs offered.

"I'm going over there tomorrow," the woman said, rather ominously from where I was sitting.

Hoo boy. This was it, I thought. Finally. The good

people of Red Lake Falls were ready to peel back the veneer of Minnesota Nice. Shit was about to get real. You expect a certain amount of gossip in a small town—the fact that everybody knows everybody else's business is one of rural life's challenges and charms. I was ready for it. But accusations of plum theft? That was something else entirely.

The couple in question, I soon learned, lived across the back alley from us, next door to the Presbyterian church. We hadn't met them because the husband, Danny, worked on gas and oil pipelines and had been off in the Dakotas for most of the summer. His wife, Missy, and their two small kids had been with them. But they had left their cat in the care of Larry, our older neighbor across the street, for the summer, and Larry had let it freely wander the neighborhood. Now they were back in town and their cat didn't want to come home.

The allegation about the plum tree was a mystery, to say the least. I had never been over to their house. The only thing I could think was that I had spent some time in the alley trimming back some of the overgrown brush from our lawn—maybe someone had seen me there and through the game of small-town telephone, "trimming brush in the alley" had transformed into "stealing plums from the neighbors"?

Later that day I told Bri about the Facebook posts and watched all the color drain from her face. She had warned me, intermittently, that the cat probably belonged to somebody else and they'd be pissed off once it stopped coming home because we were feeding it. I had pooh-poohed these concerns—if it was somebody else's cat then what the hell was it doing in our yard all day for weeks on end?

But her fears had proven justified and now we had a mess to clean up. I was prepared to let the people come over so we could tell them to go take a shit in their hats, and if their cat was so important to them they shouldn't have left it alone in the neighborhood all summer. Briana, more diplomatically minded, insisted instead on a proactive peace offering. It was late summer and she was in a baking mood, so she said she would bake them an apple pie and I would bring it over to their house and make amends. We ran the plan by Jason Brumwell to make sure it didn't violate any unspoken small-town Minnesota norms regarding neighborliness.

"Why don't you bake them a plum pie instead?" he suggested.

"This isn't funny!" Briana yelled at him.

The next day, fresh pie in hand, I embarked on the long walk from our house to Missy and Danny's. I took Jack with me based on the purely cynical calculation that a small child would help humanize the evil out-of-town reporter and that they'd be less likely to start any serious shit in his presence.

We went to the front door and I knocked. It was answered by a petite woman with long red hair.

"So uh, I'm your new neighbor and I heard that—" I began, but I didn't get a chance to finish my opening spiel.

"Yeah, look," she said. "We left the cat with Larry over the summer, okay? And he wasn't supposed to let her outside, but we found out he kept leaving her outside, and now we're back home and she won't even come see us, I guess because you've been feeding her."

"Yeah, sorry I had no idea who she belonged to!" I said. "When she started showing up we asked around but nobody seemed to know. I guess we should have asked Larry. But anyway we're sorry, we weren't trying to like, steal your cat, I promise! Briana feels really bad and she baked you a pie." I offered the pie.

"Look, kids!" Jack said. Missy's two daughters, about Jack and Charlie's age, peered out from behind her.

"Thank you," Missy said. "Could you just . . . stop feeding her?"

"Yes, of course. What's her name, by the way? She's a great cat."

"Her name's Honey."

"Honey!" one of the girls squealed.

"That's a good name for an orange cat," I said. "Maybe some time if you want, the girls could come over and play in the yard with Jack and Charlie? They love making friends in the neighborhood."

"Yeah, sure," Missy said.

And that was it. Briana's face was pressed up against our kitchen window as Jack and I walked back. "How did it go?" she asked.

"Well. Not great? But not bad, either," I said. "I told her if her kids ever wanted to come play with Jack and Charlie they were welcome to."

"Great, now they're gonna think we're trying to steal their kids, too."

That was the end, for the time being, of the Great Orange Cat Debacle of 2016. We learned our charm offensive had worked several months later when for Christmas, Missy, out of the blue, gave us four tickets to a performance of the *Nutcracker* in Grand Forks. This was surprising to me; based on our experiences in other places where we'd lived I'd assumed that Danny and Missy were now our sworn enemies and would continue to be so until we either moved away or died. When things go south with neighbors it's often impossible to put them on the right footing again. But Danny and Missy have since become good friends. Their girls come over to play with our boys in the summers, and vice versa. And in the end, oddly enough, we ended up adopting the orange cat after all. In 2017 Danny was off to West Virginia for work on the pipeline, and Missy and the girls went with him. They were gone for much of the year and Larry was put in charge of the cat again. Eventually he told them he couldn't take it anymore—it was too much of a hassle to run over to their place every day and deal with the damn cat. So they agreed to let him see if anyone else was interested, and of course when we found out, we volunteered immediately. Now the orange cat—Honey—lives with us but still spends plenty of time with Missy, Danny, and the girls when they're in town.

Other challenges began to present themselves as our Minnesota honeymoon wound down. Finding after-hours medical care out here is not so easy. The closest urgent care facility is the hospital in Grand Forks, an

Distance to nearest E.R. or urgent care (actual routes, drawn to scale)

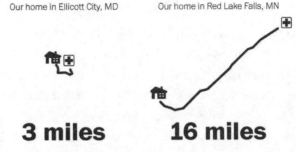

Our home in Ellicott City, MD   Our home in Red Lake Falls, MN

3 miles   **16 miles**

hour away, although we found that "urgent care" typically means just getting checked into the emergency room. One day in the fall Jack began complaining of pain when he peed. Back in Baltimore this would have been a standard urgent care call—drive out to the place around the corner, get a quick exam, and most likely be prescribed some antibiotics. Instead Briana had to take him to the emergency room in Thief River Falls, where they did the exact same procedure but we had to pay a lot more for it out of pocket due to how our health insurance is set up.

But we really didn't appreciate the medical challenges of living in a rural area until the next summer, when Jack and Charles were getting screened to enroll in preschool at the elementary school in town. We were excited to learn that the county offers universal one-day-a-week preschool. Part of the enrollment process was a standard hearing and vision screen. Charles, who had always been oddly sensitive about his ears, took great offense at having headphones placed over them and couldn't complete the screening. No worries, the staff told us, just see if you can get it done at your pediatrician's office before school starts.

The boys loved the pediatrician we had lined up for them, a Dr. Sreedharan in Thief River Falls. Charles had no problem completing the screening there but afterward Dr. S., as he told people to call him, took Briana aside.

"Has Charles ever been screened for autism?" he asked.

Dr. S. laid out the potential markers. Charles rarely made eye contact with unfamiliar people. He occasionally engaged in nontypical behaviors, like walking around the perimeter of large objects, like tables, while intently staring at them out of the corner of his eye. His cognitive abilities were quite literally off the charts—he had all his numbers memorized before the age of two. On the flip side, his expressive communication abilities were a different story. He was harder to understand, and had a much more difficult time articulating his needs, often causing him to erupt in frustration.

In the backs of our minds, we admitted to ourselves later, we had always wondered about this. Charles had lagged behind Jack on most of the big developmental milestones, like crawling and walking. Potty-training Jack had been a cinch, but Charles had been fiercely resistant to it. We knew that because they had been born six weeks prematurely they were at greater risk for autism and any number of other health problems.

Dr. Sreedharan explained that he wasn't a specialist and couldn't offer a definitive diagnosis, but it would be good to take Charles someplace where they could. There was no such facility in Thief River Falls. Ditto for Grand Forks, an hour away. The closest place was in Fargo, two hours to the south. When we called to set up an appointment, we found that they were booked out for months.

Those months, through the fall and winter of 2017, were a period of profound unease and uncertainty. If Charles was autistic, what sorts of services—speech therapy, physical therapy, and the like—would he need to live to his fullest potential, and would northwest Minnesota be able to provide them? It's one thing to move to the middle of nowhere with a healthy, self-sufficient family whose chief needs could be fulfilled by the occasional Amazon order. But how would a child with special needs fare out here? Would we be depriving him of the care he required by not living in a place like D.C. or Baltimore, where there were world-class medical facilities?

The evaluation in Fargo was less than ideal: he's not on the spectrum, they said, he's just a genius. Their "autism evaluation," as it turned out, was based largely on a written questionnaire we filled out. That wouldn't cut it as far as the school was concerned: they—and we!—wanted a rigorous clinical evaluation, which is what we thought we were going in for. The results, or lack thereof, from Fargo left us grappling with what to do next. Was there even a clinic within a thousand miles of the place that was used to dealing with kids like Charlie? Was he doomed to get written off as a "bad kid" in school just because teachers and doctors out here didn't have much experience with kids like him?

We needed another opinion. We turned to what we knew: Johns Hopkins in Baltimore.

At the Kennedy Krieger Institute's Center for Autism and Related Disorders (CARD), Charles underwent an additional two days of evaluations. He was, in fact, on the spectrum. But, as far as the doctors were concerned he'd be best off in a regular classroom with an individualized instructional plan. And he'd benefit greatly from regular speech, physical, and occupational therapy sessions to help him catch up on the skills that other kids just took for granted. The important thing at this point in his life, they stressed, was small classrooms with regular routines and familiar faces. We wanted to know if we should move back to Baltimore. Sure, they said, we could find a Maryland public school for him, but class sizes would be larger. We might be able to find a private school in Maryland that would take him on, but it would not come cheap. If we had found a great small school where he could get the assistance he needed in Minnesota, then perhaps, they suggested, we should stick with that rather than spend so much time trying to find the equivalent for Charles in Maryland.

In the years since the diagnosis, ferrying him back and forth to all those appointments—and dealing with the bills associated with them—has proven to be one of the great challenges of living here. The Pew Research Center recently reported that for the typical suburban and urban residents, the closest hospital is about a ten-minute drive away. The average rural hospital, on the other hand, is about seventeen minutes away from the average rural resident. Our nearest hospital was twenty minutes, in Thief River, but it doesn't provide any of the specialist services Charlie needs. So we've patched together a plan of care based on what's available, and what we can reach in a reasonable drive. One specialist is in Grand Forks. Another is in Crookston. One comes to the clinic in Red Lake Falls, but only periodically. Since I'm the one working, Briana bears the brunt of the ferrying duties. It's exhausting, no doubt. But then we ask ourselves: would it be any easier in Baltimore? There would probably be more options for service. But with both of us needing to work there, whoever was driving the Charlie bus would end up burning through sick time at a prodigious rate. Yes, the clinics would probably be closer. But once you factor in the traffic congestion for late afternoon appointments. the travel time would probably be similar. A ten-mile trip in suburban Maryland can easily take longer than a forty-five-mile trip in northwest Minnesota.

Once we had a diagnosis, the other big anxiety was how the community would respond. The Brumwells were the first people we told. Somehow, it was like they knew exactly what to say. Kristin Weiss, Ryan's fiancée, said simply "Oh. Well, that's his super power!" Jason quipped that he took after his father. All of them said, emphatically, that Charlie was Charlie and that this didn't change anything. It was exactly what we needed to hear.

The other wild card was the school. Would the teachers treat him differently? Was a tiny school like J. A. Hughes Elementary (typical grade size: twenty kids) be equipped to work with a kid like Charlie? Would they try to redirect him to a special ed program? We let the school know about the diagnosis, in kind of a casual "FYI" kind of manner since we didn't know what the typical protocol was. To our surprise the teachers and administrators immediately sprang into action. They bumped him up to two days a week of full-time preschool, in order to help him develop the social skills he was lacking. They worked with a special educator to put in place some in-classroom interventions, like a cool-down corner where he could take a break when he got overstimulated. They quickly performed their own evaluation, to ensure he met Minnesota state guidelines for requiring educational assistance.

Within a couple of weeks of learning about the diagnosis, the school put together a meeting between us, the principal, the pre-K teacher, a school psychologist, a special ed teacher, and a speech pathologist. They agreed that he should be in a regular classroom, on an individualized educational plan and with para-educator assistance when needed. They were extremely supportive, and to my relief and embarrassment they didn't seem to think of Charlie as a burden, or a drain on school resources. He was just a kid with a certain set of needs.

By all appearances he is currently thriving at J. A. Hughes Elementary in the town of Red Lake Falls. His kindergarten classroom is small—fifteen kids—and filled with friendly, familiar faces. As luck would have it, his kindergarten teacher, Hannah Seeger, had formerly taught special education. It is difficult to think of a more ideal environment, anywhere in the country, for a child with his specific needs than the place he is at right now. The small scale of the school drastically reduces the risk of things going south during the unstructured moments, like recess or the bus ride, that kids on the autism spectrum often have trouble with in a typical public school setting. Jason Brumwell drives the bus that picks him up for school in the morning, and Ryan drives the bus that takes him home. In larger public schools, in particular—like the ones we left behind in Maryland—kids like Charlie can easily get lost in the crowd. A special need can become a special burden, and overworked, underpaid educators can be forgiven if they don't have time to comfort a five-year-old having a meltdown because somebody else is using the crayon he wanted. Westchester Elementary, the school the boys would have attended had we stayed in Maryland, has about six hundred students. J. A. Hughes has less than a third as many. It's the kind of place where at the end of the school day, every single day, Principal Chris Bjerklie stands by the door to greet and high-five every single kid who walks out. If he can't make it, school secretary Julie Buse does it instead. In the wintertime they make sure every kid is properly attired—boots, snow pants, hat, mittens—before heading outside to face the cold.

Even with the smaller school, Charles still has his challenges, of course. He and Jack joined 4-H in kindergarten, for instance. Briana volunteers with the program, in part to keep an eye on Charlie and in part because she just enjoys helping out. One day a month they board a different bus than usual in the afternoon, which takes them to the community center in town where 4-H is held. I had some reservations about letting five-year-olds navigate an unfamiliar bus situation by themselves, but for the first few months everything went without a hitch. But then, one day in February, everything went wrong.

Jack was out sick from school that day, so the brothers wouldn't be able to look after each other the way they usually did. We found out later that Mrs. Seeger, Charlie's kindergarten teacher, was also out. So was Ryan, the usual bus driver. And on top of it all, the 4-H bus did something different that day: rather than take the 4-H kids directly to the community center it made a number of stops beforehand.

Charlie's usual support structure—brother, teacher, bus driver—wasn't in place to help him deal with the double whammy of both riding a different bus and dealing with a different route than usual on that different bus. When the bus pulled up to the community center to let the 4-H kids out, Briana realized with horror that Charlie wasn't there.

She called me. Had he gotten on his usual bus instead? No, that bus had already come and gone and he wasn't on it.

She talked to the other 4-H kids. Had Charlie been on the bus? Yes, they said. He had gotten off at an earlier stop, the one down the road. She flew out the door and ran down the road.

The temperature that day was right around zero—not too cold by northern Minnesota standards, but cold enough that a kid wandering around outside could be in some serious danger before long.

Fortunately, Charlie's snow pants are bright, Day-Glo orange—his favorite color. That was the first thing she saw, his bright orange snow pants walking down the road between two older kids. She ran up to them, breathless.

They had gotten off at the same bus stop Charlie had and he had just started walking with them, the kids said. They took him to their place and their dad, with some alarm, told them to walk him over to the county social services office, which was at the courthouse right down the road. That's what they had been doing when Bri found them.

Charles didn't seem particularly fazed by the incident, but with his expressive communication being what it was, we had a hard time figuring out his side of the story. He believed that he had gotten off the bus *after* the 4-H stop, rather than before. He saw the red brick Catholic church outside the bus and mistook it for the red brick community center. He tried to go into the church but the door was locked. He went along with the other kids because he didn't know what else to do.

It didn't end anywhere near as badly as it could have—just google "autistic child missing" for a sense of the worst-case scenarios. But it badly rattled us, and it rattled the folks at the school, too. His teacher called us. The principal called us. Jason and Ryan called us when they heard what happened. An administrator called us. Another administrator who lived in our neighborhood showed up at our door to apologize and broke down in tears.

It's hard to work out the counterfactual of how this would have played out in Baltimore schools. Would they have had five-year-olds navigating unfamiliar bus routes to begin with? Would Charlie even have been able to enroll in a regular kindergarten class with extracurricular activities? Had he gotten lost in a much larger, much stranger neighborhood, would the consequences have been much worse? Would administrators have even had time to care?

Impossible to say, in the end. What we do know is that everyone at J. A. Hughes took the incident seriously and have put in place different protocols for bus boarding to ensure something like this doesn't happen again. And when they say it won't happen again, Briana and I believe them. We can't protect a kid like Charlie from the world forever. But in a place like Red Lake Falls, he has the freedom to face a world where the scale is smaller, the faces are friendlier, and the consequences for screwups are less severe.

On the other hand, there's no question that a big school in Maryland has more to offer a bright kid than a small one in rural Minnesota. At J. A. Hughes the gym doubles as a cafeteria, and the library is used as the auditorium. There is no full-time librarian. The school shares a band teacher with the high school. Phys ed classes are mysteriously referred to as "phy ed." Sitting here it's easy to imagine all manner of wondrous, world-expanding extracurriculars that my kids are missing out on because they attend a tiny school in the middle of nowhere.

This, in fact, was one of Briana's primary concerns about moving out here. She had attended a tiny K–12 school in upstate New York—eighteen kids in her graduating class! The education she received there was substandard, at best. She was one of just four kids who went on to a four-year degree. Most of the kids simply planned to work on their parents' farms after graduation, or worse, they didn't have a plan at all. The school was poor and had little money to attract decent teachers, much less make them stick around for more than a year. Staff turnover was high. Bri had five different English teachers her senior year in high school. Most of that year was spent watching movies with various subs rather than reading real books. They didn't have Advanced Placement tests. They didn't even offer *calculus*. Briana recalls that her twelfth-grade physics teacher spent much of the class time wrestling and horsing around with the guys in her class. At the end of this year, this teacher handed another student, one of the boys who hadn't bothered to hand in any work, her lab folder. The teacher told the boy to copy what he needed from Briana's folder in order to fill out his missing work, so he wouldn't fail. Bri didn't know about any of this until after graduation.

But these drawbacks only instilled in her a desire to

rise above them all. She took advantage of every extra-curricular she could get her hands on. Some of the better teachers—and there were a few—keyed her in to life-changing experiences like Outward Bound, which made her realize the world had a lot more to offer than what Owen D. Young Central School let on. She graduated valedictorian and got accepted into Cornell. She remains pissed off, to this day, that her high school math level was so below the level other incoming freshmen received that she had to take remedial classes in her first year of college, mostly because her school didn't have enough student interest in what was considered "advanced" math.

Her principal, in fact, had made a point of telling her, during her senior year, to "get off your high horse" regarding her class ranking. Owen D. Young Central School was tiny, he said. She was just a big fish in a small pond. Compared to the other kids across New York State? She was nothing.

Nevertheless, she persisted. She made it to college, and she made it out. And she—and I—want our kids to succeed *because* of what their K–12 education offers, not in spite of it. In all honesty we don't know if the schools in Red Lake Falls can make that happen. They don't offer calculus, either. Or trigonometry. They have a robotics club, but no school paper. For the time being we're pinning our hopes on two factors.

The first is that parental involvement can pick up a lot of educational slack. A kid's success in school is largely dependent on his innate curiosity and his willingness to learn new things. That's something we can help our kids develop; it just means we'll have to take on more of the work of their education ourselves. Jack, now six, wants to play the violin, for example. There's nobody at his school who can teach him that, which means we'll have to ferry him off to lessons in Thief River or Crookston.

Looking forward, the bigger point we discovered is that high school students in the state of Minnesota are allowed to take college courses, for college credit, at a local postsecondary institution for no charge through the state's Postsecondary Enrollment Options program. If we're still here by the time Jack and Charles get into high school, and they find that the courses there aren't challenging enough, we can simply ship them off to classes at the University of Minnesota in Crookston for their junior and senior years. Our neighbors Rob and Alice told us that their son Alex took advantage of this program, and they couldn't speak highly enough of it. In addition to advanced coursework he was able to get involved in the school's music and theater programs, eventually parlaying that experience into admission to the music program at Oberlin College, one of the best music departments in the country. No such program existed in New York State when Briana was watching her physics teacher tackle her classmates in lab.

For the time being, we're at a place where we know the elementary education being offered to the boys is ideal, particularly for Charles. And we know that beyond elementary school there are more challenging instructional opportunities available to the boys, should they need it. For the moment, that's enough.

Honestly, it's a relief to not have to game out the educational arms race that so many parents grapple with on the east coast: placing your toddler in the right day care, so they can get admitted to the right pre-K program, so they can go to the right private elementary school, followed by the right prep school. It's exhausting to even contemplate the triangulation necessary to put a kid through school in that kind of environment.

When there's just one school, those concerns are largely rendered moot. As a country we've become so fixated on "choice" in our educational systems that we've forgotten how freeing it can be when you don't have to choose.

Shortly after we moved, incidentally, the Annie E. Casey Foundation published its annual rankings of the best places to grow up in America. The rankings were drawn from various official data sources, concerning things like education quality, poverty and hunger, family structure, test scores, rates of grade repetition, you name it. Minnesota came out at the absolute top of the list. "Where the children are all above average," indeed.

As summer trundled into fall our first year in Minnesota, we were feeling good about things. We had made peace with the neighbors. We were figuring out the schools, the doctors, and where to buy food. Our cupboards were stocked with applesauce made with apples from our tree in our yard, and jam made with chokecherries from another. The boys were three, somewhere between toddlers and little boys, and they were becoming easier to manage. We lived in a house that, for the first time, felt truly like home. There was space to stretch out in and fresh air to breathe. Work was going well—my output hadn't imploded since leaving the D.C. newsroom. It was refreshing to be able to log off at the end of the workday, to step away from the social media madness of the news cycle and into a home life that was more grounded, more solid, in many ways more real.

It felt like we were getting everything we had hoped for when we first moved. Yet somehow, it felt like something was missing. We couldn't quite put our finger on it. The feeling didn't express itself as a lack, or a shortcoming, necessarily, but rather as a space for something more. Space that had never even been imaginable back in Maryland.

Briana blames me for suggesting what came next, and I blame her. Regardless, whichever one of us gave voice to it first didn't face much opposition from the other: "What if we tried for a girl?"

Throughout the twins' infancy we had made dark jokes about having another kid, usually during the most trying moments. One memorable day in Maryland, for instance, both twins had been sick, the drain hose to the washing machine had come undone, flooding the basement, and the dog had eaten something he shouldn't have and was alternately puking and shitting all over the house. "At least we don't have triplets!" we would say at times like those.

But we had never seriously entertained the thought of another kid in Maryland. We were barely getting by with just two of them. We, evidently, were not alone.

The U.S. fertility rate has been on a long, steady decline, from nearly ninety births per woman age fifteen to forty-four in 1970 to about sixty in 2017. A lot of that decline is due to things worth applauding: expanded access to abortion and contraceptive services, and greater autonomy for women and men to decide whether and how to have kids.

But economic pressures are playing a role in this, too. Middle-class wages have stagnated. Housing has become staggeringly expensive, particularly in coastal urban areas. Day-care and educational costs are skyrocketing. And among the world's wealthy nations, the United States remains a stubborn outlier when it comes to policies like paid parental work leave (the United States doesn't mandate any) and universal child care (ditto). In many states, day care is now more expensive than a college education.

Those competing pressures have made it more difficult than ever to have kids, and Americans aren't exactly happy about it. Data from the U.S. Centers for Disease Control and Prevention (CDC) and the General Social Survey show, for instance, that the gap between how many children women say they want to have (2.7 on average) and how many they'll actually have (1.8, on average) is the highest it's been in forty years.

If you want to be strictly utilitarian about it, you might say that policy makers have pursued such an aggressive probusiness agenda over the past forty years that they've overlooked the question of whether parents will be able to afford to continue producing the customers who will buy stuff from those businesses in the future. To be more blunt, as a country we've pursued economic policies that are good for corporations and their shareholders, but lousy for their employees and their families.

We weren't interested in producing another future Wal-Mart customer, of course. But we suddenly found ourselves in a place where we had the time, the money, the space, the community support, and the love to bring another life into the world. Given my own anti-kid past, I'm not the kind of person to go around insisting that people who don't want kids will someday change their minds, or that people who already have kids secretly want more. But our own experience does make me wonder how many other couples might not realize that, given the right circumstances, there could be space for more children, more love, in their own lives?

The big thing we were worried about was the possibility of another set of twins—or worse. Parents who have twins once are more likely to have twins if they get pregnant again. At Johns Hopkins, where the twins were born, Briana's doctor told a story one day about a couple who had twins—two boys—and then decided to try for a girl. They ended up getting pregnant with triplets, and subsequently found out that all three would be boys. The parents left the office sobbing that day.

We decided to go for it, though. Briana was pregnant within two months of going off birth control. We were greatly relieved to discover that this time there would be just one baby. Our Minnesota child was on the way.

CHAPTER 7

It's 9 a.m. on a crisp northern Minnesota fall morning. I'm standing in the driveway of a Red Lake County farmhouse, decked out head to toe in hand-me-down blaze orange from the Brumwell brothers. There's a dead deer hanging from the raised bucket of a tractor in front of me. It isn't mine. Two or three guys with knives circle around it, slicing downward through gut and tendon to remove the hide.

They eventually give it a mighty tug, stripping it clear of the back and rear haunches until it remains attached only at the shanks. One final heave and the hide drops to the ground with a plop. The carcass steams in the morning sun. The farmer's dog looks up briefly from the severed foreleg it's been chewing on, and then gets back to business.

"Now that's Minnesota deer season," Dick Brumwell, who's been overseeing the whole operation, announces with a grin.

It was the opening of deer season in 2016, November 5, three days before the election. We'd been out since well before dawn, part of the local hunting party that the Brumwells have been a part of for decades. I'd shivered alone in the indigo predawn hours, listening to the birds wake up around me. I didn't see a single sign of a deer myself, which was just as well—after the group reconvened at the house in midmorning I realized that I'd forgotten to even load the rifle the Brumwells loaned me.

My own dad loved guns. He was a champion skeet shooter as a kid, and went target shooting all his life. But as a veterinarian he preferred healing animals to shooting them. As a result, while I'd shot the occasional handgun in the course of my life, I'd never been deer hunting before, much less fired a gun at an animal. The Brumwells were determined to change that.

Hunting's on the wane across America. Since 1980 the national population has grown by one hundred million, while the number of people hunting each year has slowly dwindled. Urbanization has taken its toll.

But the hunt is still huge in northwest Minnesota. Statewide nearly half a million people go hunting each year, five times as many as back in Maryland. Even if you didn't hunt it would be impossible to miss deer season up here. Once the season opens it's hard to drive a block in town without seeing a deer carcass hanging from a tree, waiting to be butchered.

Dick Brumwell and his buddy Russ Coenen, a retired high school science teacher, had been hunting the same patch of Russ's land religiously, every single year since the 1970s. As soon as Dick's kids were old enough to get a hunting license they started going out with him. As a born-again Minnesotan the Brumwells were adamant that I experience the hunt for myself. For starters that meant getting my own license. Because I'd never had one in Minnesota before, I had to take an online hunting safety course intended for teenage hunters. I had to sit through several hours of videos full of idiotic safety tips, like "do not point the gun at yourself," and then take a test afterward. Ryan and Jason thought it was hilarious. I demonstrated my on-paper hunting prowess by scoring a 92.

Now that I was qualified to haul a rifle through the woods, the next step was target practice. The brothers planned a special treat: one afternoon in late October, Ryan picked up several pounds of Tannerite from a hunting supply store in Thief River. Tannerite's an explosive that only ignites when it gets hit with a fast-moving gun round. You can pour it, shake it, throw it around, no problems. But when you shoot it, it explodes. You can find YouTube videos of guys (yes, almost always guys) stuffing old cars and appliances full of Tannerite and then nearly getting beheaded by a flying door or wheel.

We were going to stuff it into pumpkins.

"Does that really sound like a smart idea to you?" Briana asked as I geared up to join the brothers down at the campground.

"No," I said, "but I kind of have to do this. It's part of my Minnesota education."

"It's fucking stupid is what it is," she said. "Did you see the video of the guy who blew his leg off with a lawn mower full of this stuff?"

"Yeah," I said. "It's just pumpkins, though. Worst that'll happen is I get hit with a flying stem."

"Right through your eyeball and it would serve you right," she said.

In all honesty it was kind of amazing to me that you can just walk into a store and buy the stuff by the bucketload, with no special permits needed, no placement on a government watch list. But I went down to the campground, where the Brumwell boys had already laid out a veritable arsenal—handguns, long guns, everything in between.

"Pour this into that pumpkin over there," Ryan said. He handed me a bottle of Tannerite, thousands of tiny white pellets, like mini mothballs.

"Why aren't you doing it?"

"I don't feel like losing a hand today."

"It won't explode unless you shoot it, right?"

"Sure."

I filled the pumpkin up to the top. Once I'd placed it on the ground, the Brumwells handed me a rifle. "This is the one I used when I was a kid," Ryan said. "Should be just right for you." They showed me where the safety was, showed me how to load it, sat me down at a picnic table, then told me to point it at the pumpkin and pull the trigger.

"You sure this is legal?" I said. "I mean there's houses right over there."

"We're just outside town limits; anything goes out here," Jason said. "Pull that trigger, find out what freedom feels like."

I inhaled. Exhaled slightly. Held. I pulled the trigger.

The sound was cataclysmic. My understanding of gunfire acoustics is drawn primarily from video games, where small guns go "pew-pew" and big ones go "BOOM-BOOM." I was expecting a pew but the rifle BOOMed. Almost instantaneously there was a second, even louder report as the pumpkin exploded in a cloud of yellow smoke. Chunks of orange meat rained down, seeds flying everywhere with pumpkin gobs attached.

The Brumwells hooted and hollered. I hooted and hollered with them.

"Gotta tell you—I thought there was no way you'd hit it on the first shot," Ryan said.

"Yeah, well, I did score a ninety-two on that test," I said. "Hope you're not mad when I bring home a bigger buck than you."

The season started off inauspiciously, however. My alarm didn't go off on the day of, which meant Ryan had to bang on our door for ten minutes at five o'clock in the morning to wake me up, and then wait around another fifteen minutes while I rushed through the house gathering my gear for the day. That subsequently made us late to meet Jason and Dick at Jason's house, and the three of them chewed me out up one side and down another all the way on the drive out to Russ's property.

Once at Russ's, the brothers and I hopped on a four-wheeler and took a bumpy ten-minute ride through the pitch darkness, across fields and through oak woods to the stand they had decided to post me at. I didn't find out until later that it was by far the worst stand out of the dozen or so on Russ's property, being located near a dirt road and far away from any of the well-trod deer paths.

The brothers dropped me off at the stand, armed with their old rifle and a five-round magazine, bristling with cartridges that looked large enough to take down a small aircraft. Jason sent me off with a thermos of coffee, black.

And with that the brothers tore off to their respective stands.

Before I go any further I should probably clarify what "deer stand" means in Minnesota. Where I'm from, in upstate New York, a deer stand is basically a couple of planks nailed to a tree at a haphazard angle, most likely constructed under the influence of alcohol. Six people died of hunting mishaps in New York State during the 2017 deer season. Just one involved a gun. The rest involved tumbles from tree stands.

A deer stand in northwest Minnesota, by contrast, is more properly understood as a small dwelling. Nearly all the stands on Coenen's property that year, for instance, were free-standing structures. I helped the Brumwells set up a new stand there prior to the start of the season. It towered above the ground on a base of four-by-four pressure-treated timber posts. It had four square walls and a sloped roof, precision-engineered by Dick back at the workshop at the campground. From each wall, a sliding Plexiglas bus window provided a commanding view of the surrounding terrain. The interiors of the walls were covered with foam insulation board, to keep the chill out, while the exterior was clad in vinyl siding. Two large northern Minnesota men could sit comfortably in the cabin side by side. The flooring extended several feet beyond one of the walls to provide a sort of patio.

But the Brumwells' stands were downright spartan

compared to some of the other options locals spring for. There are companies that sell luxurious molded plastic or fiberglass structures with upward of eight sides to ensure an optimal shooting angle no matter which way the deer approach from. They resemble nothing more than World War II pillboxes on stilts. Russ himself had one of these, erected at the top of a hill with sight lanes cut through the forest at every angle for maximum visibility.

As the new man in the group I was afforded none of these luxuries, although my stand was still a palace by upstate New York standards. It was at least a decade old and accessed via a rickety hatch in the floor. When I stationed myself within it, perched on a folding chair, each of the four walls was just inches from my body. It was insulated with scraps of foamboard presumably left over from more lavish projects, but most of them were falling off the walls, gnawed for years by whatever rodents I heard skittering about the structure as I settled myself in for the morning. The windows were aluminum-framed rejects from one of the campground buses and most of them appeared to be wedged shut. I managed to open one just a crack, producing a screeching sound that was certain to scare off any mammals within a three-hundred-yard radius. Due to the cramped quarters I had difficulty finding an angle to lean my rifle that didn't end up pointing the muzzle toward my face. The Brumwells had lent me a portable propane heater, which, they assured me, was safe to use in close quarters and presented no danger of asphyxiation by carbon monoxide. I was nervous about using it, but even with the unseasonable warmth that day—it was about 30 degrees—eventually the chill became so intense that I had little choice. Orange waves of sublimating propane radiated across the surface of the heater. I was terrified to move, lest I accidentally catch a bit of cloth on it and send the entire structure up in flames.

Still, after some time I began to relax, watching the inky black sky turn purple and eventually a deep navy blue. Around the time the birds began to wake, the silence started to be punctuated by distant rifle shots, rich and booming, like fireworks heard from a distance. The hunt was on.

Judging by the thunderous reports coming in it sounded as if hunters were picking off deer in every direction. But as the sky continued to lighten I still hadn't seen a single one. I fidgeted in my seat, craning my neck toward all four windows. Not so much as a squirrel rustling in the underbrush. Suddenly I heard an unidentifiable noise. It sounded like something big. I froze, felt my muscles tense, reached for my rifle. I held it close and continued to listen. There it was again! It was a moo. *A fucking moo.* The cows at the nearby farm were waking up. I sank back into my seat.

By this point I had to take a leak something fierce. Figured I may as well make my way down to ground level and stretch my legs. Problem: it was so cramped in the stand that I couldn't figure out how to open the hatch beneath me, which took up almost the entire floor, without somehow wedging myself between the walls and dangling above it, Spider-Man style. After spending twenty minutes repeatedly shifting myself, the heater, the chair, and the gun around in the stand, like one of those awful sliding tile puzzles with only one free space, I gave up on trying to climb down and instead decided I'd straddle the hatch, wedge it open as best I could, and simply take a whizz through it. That way, I reasoned, I wouldn't have to deal with repeating the whole process in reverse once I was done.

I finished up, closed the hatch, and just managed to get myself settled again when I heard the four-wheeler rumbling down the trail. Jason and Ryan were coming to pick me up. After a good deal of fumbling I managed to worm my way down through the hatch. As I descended toward the ground I was puzzled to find that the ladder rungs were wet. Then I realized that I had peed on them.

Jason and Ryan regaled me with tales of the giant bucks they'd seen but decided not to fire on.

"Saw about thirty doe and an eight-pointer but he looked scrawny," Jason said.

"Little six-pointer came by and rubbed his antlers on the base of my stand," Ryan said. "No point in wasting my tag on him."

"I didn't see shit," I said.

"That's because you slept in too late," Jason said.

We went back to the farmhouse, where Russ and the rest of the crew were dismembering the deer one of them had shot. For Russ, the hunt wasn't so much about bagging deer as it was about making venison sausage. He had an enormous smoker set up in his barn. As the deer came in he and an old friend would process the meat, running it through a massive grinder alongside a generous portion of pork and some spices. They'd run the mixture through casing, tie it off, and hang it in the smoker for hours. While he waited for the deer to come in, Russ fretted with the smoker, ensuring that the moist wood chips at the bottom were putting off just the optimal amount of smoke at the precise temperature. When the season's sausage making was done he would vacuum-pack them and distribute them to members of the party and stockpile mountains of the stuff for himself.

Dick loves the hunt. He remarked several times that day that "hunting would be a lot more fun if it weren't for the damn deer." He loves the hunt, just not necessarily the gory bits involving the shooting and the cleaning and whatnot. But he likes being outdoors, alone in a stand, just him and his thoughts and the wild prairie around him.

People living in cities pay thousands of dollars to psychiatrists, spiritual healers, and meditation gurus to learn how to cleanse their minds and achieve just a few moments of inner peace. Dick does it every year for a week in November for no more than the cost of a Minnesota deer license. If he happens to bag a deer, well, that's just something to piss and moan about to his buddies at the end of the day.

"All right," Russ announced after about an hour of BS'ing with the group in the barn, "time to walk the woods."

"What are we doing now?" I whispered to Jason as everyone trudged out of the barn and toward the fleet of ATVs and farm vehicles idling nearby. Nobody had bothered briefing me on what a full day of deer hunting actually looked like.

"We're walking," Jason said, "through the woods. Is there something about that that's confusing?"

"So like, just walking through the woods looking for deer? Like, all of us?"

"This is *deer* hunting you signed up for, so yes."

"And so like what, if we see a deer we shoot it?"

"Yes, that's what the goddamn gun is for or haven't you been paying attention? Did they not cover this in your junior hunter's certification class?"

The vehicles reconvened atop a slight rise, where Russ had a big tract of open field bordered by a shallow wood. All of us lined up at the edge of the wood, spaced twenty or so yards apart. As I walked over I let the muzzle end of my rifle dip too low for Dick's liking. "Point that goddamn thing somewhere else!" he snapped.

"It's not loaded!" I protested.

"Every gun's loaded," he snapped. Fair enough.

"So when they say 'go,'" Jason explained, "we all walk forward through the woods. Stay parallel with the guys on either side of you. Don't get too far ahead or behind, or you'll get shot if a deer jumps out in front of you."

I adjusted my orange cap so it was sticking up as high as possible. "That seems dange—"

"GO!" someone yelled. Everyone crashed forward directly through the underbrush. There were no trails;

we waded through thickets of scrub and felled trees. "Hey, deer!" people yelled, hoping to scare up some game. "Ho, deer!"

I was falling behind, stumbling through the brush, unable to find my footing. Branches snapped at my face, vines grabbed at my boots. I looked up and couldn't see anyone to either side but it seemed the rustling of leaves and crackling of branches were everywhere. A gunshot rang out somewhere ahead of me.

"Shit!" I yelled.

I heard Ryan a few yards ahead. "Get up here, Ingraham." I careened forward and suddenly I was out in the open again, blinking in the cold morning sun.

"Jesse saw a deer running along the tree line on the opposite side of the field," Jason explained. "Took a shot but no luck. If you had kept up you would have known this."

"I'd be happy never doing that again," I said.

"Good, we've got about five more woods to walk today."

And we did. As the sun reached higher and the air got hotter our motley caravan crisscrossed Russ's land, hitting every major tract of woods on it. We trundled down into little valleys carved by streams and hiked across recently tilled fields through clumps of rich black dirt as big as your boot. At one point the group split up: one contingent would walk through a chunk of woods, and the rest of us would take up posts outside it, ready to fire on any deer they rustled up. "If you shoot, shoot north," Dick said. "Don't need anybody shooting at me today."

"Where do you want me to post?" I asked.

"You're gonna need to post on the eastern edge of the field, by the neighbor lady's house."

"The one who doesn't like hunting?"

"Yep."

Russ had evidently had some sort of hunting-related altercation with the neighbor some years earlier, and as a result they weren't on the best of terms. To reach my assigned spot, I would basically have to walk half the perimeter of her property, in full view of her house the entire time.

I made my walk with my head held high and my rifle leaning responsibly across the shoulder, just an upstanding young hunter doing his part to control the deer population and certainly *not* looking to aggravate any nonhunters by dint of my presence or behavior. As I walked by the section of fence closest to the neighbor's house a door opened, and I saw a woman standing in the doorway, arms folded. I gave a big wave and smiled my best smile, trying to appear as nonthreatening as a strange man with a long gun can appear. She shook her head and went back in the house. I finally reached my post. I saw that the other guys had already flushed out their woods and hadn't found anything. Everyone was already heading on to the next section. I turned around and walked all the way back the way I came.

Regrouping back at the barn, the party enjoyed a late lunch of ground venison chili cooked by Russ's wife, Inez. I know I've spent a considerable number of pages of this book complaining about Minnesota food but this chili was *phenomenal*. Easily among the best I've ever had. One reason? The chili's chief ingredients—the tomatoes, onions, carrots, and peppers from Inez's garden, and the deer from Russ's woods—had all been harvested directly from the very land we were sitting on.

After lunch it was time to hit the stands again to catch the evening movement of the deer. Since a few guys had already gotten their bucks there was some shuffling of stands going on, with the net result that I got to sit in a different stand that was less of a piece of shit than the one I'd had in the morning. The stand overlooked a food plot of soybeans, which the Brumwells assured me would be Grand Central for deer once the sun started sinking. The stand was a little bigger so I could maneuver around in it more easily, and the windows actually worked so I could crack them open and practice poking the barrel of my rifle out of them in quick succession. I looked at birds through my scope and practiced loading and unloading the chamber of the rifle, and attaching and detaching the five-round magazine. Still, no deer showed up. I considered trying to vaporize a sparrow to practice my aim but decided against it, realizing that the Brumwell brothers would hear the shot and give me hell for wasting their ammunition on a bird. So I continued waiting, until darkness, when their four-wheeler pulled up to bring me home. Still no deer.

"Well," Jason said as we got back into his car. "Same time tomorrow?"

I thought about this. That night the clocks would turn back, meaning that Ryan would need to show up at my house at 4 a.m., which meant that I'd need to be up by at least three thirty to avoid another late start.

There was no way I'd be able to do it and I told them as much. Way too goddamn early, I said, to sit shivering in a box and wait for some hypothetical deer to show up. They howled and gave me hell all the way home. The only thing worse than being late for the hunting party, apparently, was deciding to bow out of it the next day. I stood firm. I wasn't about to leave Briana home with the twins for another full day, I said. I'd wait until the following weekend. I'd come out for one afternoon. I'd sit in the stand in the evening but no way in hell would I be doing another round of woods walking. I stood firm. If I didn't get a deer then, well, it wasn't meant to be.

Fine, they said. Get out of here. We're gonna bag the biggest goddamn bucks anyone's ever seen tomorrow and you'll hear all about it.

Thus ended my first day of deer hunting.

That year, 2016, was a mild autumn in northwest Minnesota. The colors changed, a chill crept up the river valleys, and the tempo of life sped up a little for the harvest. Trucks barreled down dirt roads carrying hauls of wheat, corn, and soybeans. Combines and tractors worked the fields at all hours of the day and night, lights shining and engines rumbling under the clear moon.

But autumn is fleeting here, too. In 2017 there was a thick blanket of snow on the ground by Halloween, and the landscape wasn't completely clear of snow again until the following May. In 2018 we got our first snow in late September, less than one week after the last official day of summer.

That first fall I realized, with some chagrin, that I'd have to deal with leaf maintenance and removal in a much more serious way than I'd ever had to before. We've got a number of huge oak trees on our property and in September they dump prodigious amounts of brown leafy biomass on the grass below. I did some research and found out that in some cases you could simply mulch up the leaves with your lawn mower and leave them there until spring.

Perfect, I thought. I'll just run the mower across the lawn a couple of times in the fall and that'll be it. No raking, no bagging, no hauling off to the dump. Christopher Ingraham's momma didn't raise no fool.

In early October, when about half the oak leaves had fallen, I took the mower out and made a pass through the leaves. In my mind's eye, the leaves would disintegrate into brown specks that settled on the dirt around the blades of grass, creating a nutrient-rich mulch that would nurture them the following spring. But when I looked back at the path of destruction behind me, I realized that my lawn was now simply covered in ragged chunks of leaf material rather than whole leaves. In another couple of weeks the leaves would bury the property completely, and if I left them there the grass would be dead come spring.

This was discouraging.

So I sat and thought. Well, I reasoned, the chief hassle of removing leaves is the bagging. Perhaps I can skip that step by simply raking all the leaves toward the garden and piling them up in there. They'll decay by spring, leaving behind a nutrient-rich mulch that would nurture the garden the following year.

The next weekend I got out my rake and began the laborious work of gathering all the leaf litter toward the garden on the edge of the property. Our neighbor John, who owns approximately six thousand pieces of heavy equipment, each tailored to any specific task that might need to be done at home or on the farm, was happily trucking around his lawn on his ride-on mower with an oversize vacuum attachment that hoovered up the leaves and deposited them into three pre-bagged bins on the back.

Hah, I thought to myself as I heaved piles of leaves over the garden fence. No need for *me* to spend hundreds of dollars on a lawn mower accessory I'll use once a year.

John drove the mower over by where I was working.

"Whatcha doin' there?" he asked.

"Well," I said, "I'm gonna put all the leaves in the garden and let them decompose over winter, and then use them as mulch in the spring."

John narrowed his eyes and slowly shook his head. "Nope," he said. "Those leaves ain't gonna break down."

"Sure they will," I said.

"You know how cold it gets here in the winter? You think anything's gonna break down when it's below zero for three months straight? You'd have better luck sticking them in your freezer."

I hadn't considered this. The truth of what he was saying became obvious to me immediately. But half the leaves were in the garden already. I couldn't stop now.

"Well. We'll see I guess!" I said, not wanting to admit the fatal flaw in my brilliant plan.

"You sure?" he said. "You can borrow my mower when I'm done if you want. Pull up all the leaves nice and easy."

"Nope," I said. It was a matter of pride now. You could bury me in those goddamn leaves before I'd accept anyone's help with them. "No, I'll be good. Thanks, though."

Next spring the leaves were still there. We didn't end up planting a garden that year, so the pile overwintered another year. And guess what? They were still there in 2018, too. That fall I officially gave up and hired a professional lawn service to do the mowing. The guy came out to do an estimate.

"You want me to haul away that pile of leaves in the garden there?" he asked.

I still couldn't admit defeat. "No," I said. "I like them there."

Briana called him back the next day. "Will you please take away the pile of leaves in the garden?" she asked. "We'll pay you whatever it takes. Yes, I know what my husband said. You need to understand he has a problem and he needs somebody to do this for him. Yes, thank you."

The next day, the leaves were finally gone.

John also gave me a crash course in the fundamentals

of the sugar beet harvest that year. You may think, as I did, that you have some idea of what a sugar beet is, but take it from me: you have absolutely no clue. A sugar beet resembles one of the dinky purple beets you grow in your garden the same way that a Sherman tank resembles a Honda Civic. The median sugar beet is the size of a large child's head and perfectly white. They're typically a foot long and weigh anywhere from three to five pounds. You know those weird white vegetables that Mario yanks out of the ground in *Super Mario Bros. 2*, the ones that are half the size he is? That's the most accurate depiction of a sugar beet ever produced by popular culture.

In the eighteenth century the sugar beet's predecessors were fed to cattle before somebody realized the beets contained sucrose, the same stuff that makes sugarcane sweet. A few centuries of selective breeding produced those fat, sweet monsters that farmers plant today. At roughly 20 percent pure sugar, a single beet can yield up to a pound or so of refined sugar.

You probably think that most of the table sugar you consume at home and in restaurants comes from sugarcane. You're wrong. Between 55 and 60 percent of it actually comes from sugar beets, according to the U.S. Department of Agriculture. You think that most of the stuff you sprinkle into your coffee comes from tropical plantations, but most of it is grown in the mainland United States, in places like the Red River valley on the border between North Dakota and Minnesota.

About thirteen thousand years ago, an area of North America roughly the size of the Black Sea was covered by a glacial lake called Lake Agassiz. For thousands of years, the lake's animal inhabitants ate, pooped, and died in its waters, depositing a thick layer of organic material along its bottom. When the glaciers receded the lake drained, fairly rapidly, leaving all that material behind as beautiful black soil and raising global sea levels anywhere from two to nine feet in the process. As a result the Red River valley's farmland is some of the most productive in the entire world, despite the short growing season of the northern climate.

In addition to your staples like corn, wheat, and soybeans, the soft soil makes for ideal beet-growing conditions. When October comes the beets are ready for harvest, and every last person in the area knows it on account of the hundreds of semi-trucks laden with tons of beets that go barreling down the country roads at this time of year.

In 2016 John took me out on the harvest one afternoon. We met at the grain elevator in the town of Euclid, northwest of Red Lake County on U.S. Route 75. John's job was to pick up the freshly harvested beets from the field and haul them several miles away to one of the holding stations operated by American Crystal Sugar. There the beets would be weighed and then piled and left to sit out in the cold until the big processing stations in East Grand Forks and Crookston were ready to take them.

I assumed that there would be some sort of large piece of beet-holding equipment along the side of the road that John would drive up to, and it would dump the load of beets in his trailer. Instead he wheeled the semi, trailer and all, directly into the field and pulled up alongside the massive treaded beet harvester that was waiting. When the harvester started up, John had to drive through the dirt alongside it, maintaining a constant distance and pace so the beets tumbling off the machine's conveyer dropped into the trailer. He also had to keep an eye on his mirror to make sure the beets weren't piling too high in any one part of the trailer. If they were, he had to speed up or slow down as necessary to ensure they were being distributed evenly.

If you're wondering how an eighteen-wheeler laden with twenty tons of beets drives through a soft field without getting stuck, the answer is it doesn't. Things usually start to get dodgy near the end of a pass through the field, when the truck and the harvester have to turn around. The truck is almost bound to lose traction, so what happens is he gets a tow from a guy in an enormous tractor outfitted with treads. The tractor has a tow hitch on the back and the truck has a matching bar on the front for just this purpose. The tractor backs into the truck with a thud, the hitch grabs the bar, and the trucker gets a quick 180-degree tow so he can start the process all over again. Once the trailer is full the trucker drives off the field and the next truck waiting in line takes its turn.

The trucks end up absolutely covered in dirt, and deposit enormous amounts of the stuff on the roadways during this season. Locals like to bitch about the beet dirt but none of them really mean it; lots of dirt means a good harvest and money in the pockets of the farmers, the truck drivers, the processing plant workers, and all their families.

Once we had a load full of beets, John drove us out to the receiving station. There he stopped to get his truck weighed and the weight recorded, and to tease the girl behind the weigh station window about this thing and that thing. Once that was done he'd pull up alongside an enormous conveyor belt. The different components of the belt would swing into place at the dump end of the trailer, and John would lift the trailer and dump all the beets out the back. We'd watch them roll up the conveyor belts, and at the top get flung out onto the massive beet mountains that eventually end up covering the entire receiving station grounds. Once the load was empty he'd go do it again, dozens of times a day, until the field was fully harvested or he needed to take a break. Pitching in with the harvest for a few days is a good way for a guy with a truck to make an extra thousand bucks or so before the winter finally sets in.

Another sign that autumn is in full swing is the presence of corn shocks in people's front yards, particularly out in the country. Dick Brumwell taught us the term for the bundles of standing cornstalks tied near the top with twine, usually accompanied by some decorative gourds and straw bales.

"Corn shocks," he said.

"Corn *stalks*?" we asked.

"Corn *shocks*. What in the hell's the matter with you

east coasters anyway?" Dick couldn't bear the thought of us spending our first fall in Minnesota without a proper shock gracing our yard. So he brought us out to his expansive garden down by the river, where some of his corn plants grew ten or twelve feet high.

"All right, chop off some of these and drag 'em over to your car. I'll go get you some pumpkins."

Bri and I set about hacking at the thick stalks with knives and pruning shears while Jack and Charles chased each other through the rows. We eventually ended up with a pile that looked like it would fill our CRV to the brim, just barely leaving enough room for the boys. Dick came back over.

"All right, that's a good bundle," he said. "Now go get three more of those."

We protested, but he told us to shut the hell up since we didn't know what we were doing, and that he'd bring anything that didn't fit in the car over to our place on his Prowler.

In the end we stood all the stalks up in our yard and tied them together near the top. The final shock was generally the shape of a tall triangle with a bunch of tassels springing out of the top. It was kind of like a fall version of a Christmas tree. Dick, we later learned, was particularly fond of corn shocks because it was a project that he and his late wife, Diane, had always done with their children around this time of year. We were glad he could show us how to carry on the tradition.

We were surprised to find most people pulled their shocks down shortly after Halloween.

"That's stupid," I said. "They should stay up until at least Thanksgiving, add a bit of cheer to November."

"They probably take them down because they freeze in place and then you're stuck with them until the spring," Bri said. "You should go take ours down while we still can."

"Like hell I will," I said. "Look how seasonal and goddamn festive that is. I'll take it down after Thanksgiving, when we put the Christmas stuff up."

"Don't you think these Minnesotans might understand this a little better than you, seeing as how this is our first fall here?"

"These people don't even know how to cook venison," I said. "They don't have a monopoly on all things autumnal. We're gonna teach them a few things, you watch."

The next weekend it snowed and the temperatures plunged well below freezing, not to return again until spring. The corn shock was rooted in place, as were the straw bales and gourds, which were now also solid as a rock. The arrangement remained there all winter, mocking me as the snow piled around it.

"What do you think is decaying faster," Bri asked in January, "the pumpkins in the front yard or the pile of leaves in the garden?"

I said nothing.

With a beet harvest and a proper corn shock under my belt there remained one item on my Minnesota bucket list before fall was out: I still wanted to bag my first deer. In the week following my disastrous first foray into the field, Ryan had swung by one evening, grinning from ear to ear, with a ten-point buck strapped to a trailer behind his car.

"See?" he said. "This is what you miss out on when you don't show up to hunt."

"Show me proof you didn't just hit it with your car."

"Go fuck yourself, Ingraham." He drove off.

Jason got himself a deer, too, an even bigger buck, a twelve-pointer in fact. I told them I wanted to go one more time, set myself up in a stand on Russ's property some afternoon. The next weekend was the last weekend of the season so it would have to be then. That Saturday the Brumwells again drove me out to Russ's property. Dick was already there; he'd bagged a deer earlier in the week but kept going out to the stands just because he enjoyed it so much. As we readied ourselves for my final attempt he told a tale about some deer he had watched out in one of the fields that morning.

"Well, there's this group of doe grazing in the field," he says, "and along comes this young buck, little guy, maybe six points, looked like he had a tine missing on one of his antlers. Well, he comes over to the does all puffed out but they want nothing to do with him, they keep running off and you can tell he's getting agitated. Well, finally this great big older buck, this experienced old man, walks slowly over to him and nods his head at him, like he's calming the young guy down. Telling him to take it easy, he's still young, he's got lots of time, no need to be in a hurry and rush things. Well, what do you know, eventually the two of them go walking off together, just quietly out of the field side by side. It was the neatest goddamn thing, I tell ya."

Once again we load up the Prowler. This time they give me a prime location—Jason's new stand that I'd help put together earlier in the season, the one with the porch overlooking the corn plot.

"If you can't find a deer here, Ingraham, I don't know what to tell you," Ryan says.

I climb up the ladder, get comfy in the seat, luxuriate in the space. I slide the windows open and shut just for the hell of it; they're quiet as a whisper. I check my rifle; there's a round in the chamber and the magazine's attached. I've got six shots if I need them.

The sun goes down and there's nothing moving in the corn except for a few birds. I'm about to write the whole thing off, convinced that these sonofabitching Brumwells have probably been spraying my stands with deer repellant before I get there as a joke, when suddenly I see them: a whole herd of deer making their way into the feed plot.

I look them over from my tower: doe, doe, doe, all doe. They have no idea I'm here. It's silent, you can hear their footsteps, the rustling of the cornstalks as they pass. They're in no hurry, ambling casually about the corn. Some of the deer on the edge of the group look up from time to time with a wary eye but there's no sense of hurry about them. Hunting season is almost over; the deer that are still here have nearly guaranteed themselves another trip around the sun.

I see a slightly larger deer emerge from the edge of

opposite direction. They'd had to put Jack back on the CPAP. They'd tried to feed Charlie orally but he choked. Then the rules were strict, the road to discharge foggy and uncertain. Sometimes one of them would have a good night while the other regressed, and those were the most confusing days of all.

There is only one question on any parent's mind during a child's NICU stay: when can my baby come home? But the doctors and nurses there don't think like that. They're fixated on the moment, on the vital signs, on the numbers flashing on the screen. It's not clear to me whether the staff at Hopkins were specifically trained not to offer any long-term prognoses to anxious parents, or whether, due to intense, highly specialized training and a laser focus on the here and now, they were simply no longer capable of thinking about time in linear terms. As a result you, the parent, become incapable of thinking that way, too. You become tethered to the moment. Time disappears. The NICU stall where your baby is becomes your whole world. Lights on a screen, the soft whoosh of a ventilator, tiny cries heard off in the distance. Afterward, if you're one of the fortunate parents who gets to bring their baby home, you can no longer tell whether your NICU time was measured in hours or days or months. There's a black void in your memory that you stay far away from because you know, beyond doubt, that it encompasses the absolute worst days of your life.

Four years after Jack and Charlie's NICU stay ended I was standing in the office with Briana asking her what we were supposed to do now. We both struggled not to panic. The kids were running around upstairs, unaware anything was amiss. We hadn't packed an overnight bag. We'd barely discussed what we'd do with Jack and Charles when it was time to deliver, although at one point Ryan Brumwell and his girlfriend, Kristin, told us they'd be happy to take the boys on short notice when the time came.

So we called Ryan. No answer. Kristin. No answer. We tried Jason. No answer. Curse these Minnesotans and their perpetual industriousness! We called Dick. He answered. We told him what was happening. "I'll be right there," he said. Less than five minutes later, he was.

When he saw the looks on our faces he immediately understood the gravity of the situation. We tried to give him a crash course in everything the twins could conceivably need that evening. "Shut the fuck up and don't worry about it!" he said. "Just go!"

"What's the matter with Momma?" Jack asked as he saw us preparing to leave.

"Momma's sick, we have to go to the doctor," I told him. "Be good for Mr. Dick and listen to what he tells you." He and Charles fidgeted anxiously in the doorway. They could tell something was terribly wrong.

We raced down the county highways toward Crookston, past fields covered with a fresh coat of snow from the night before. Briana was breathing hard, straining. The contractions were very close. I tried to keep up a steady patter of reassurances for both of us—we've been through this before, there's only one this time, he'll be bigger, he'll be healthier.

"I can't do this again," she said.

"Yes, we can," I said. "We have to."

In truth I felt the same way she did. When we'd found out we were having just one baby this time, the first words out of my mouth were "Well, no matter what else happens we won't have to go to that goddamned NICU again." Now we were headed toward a NICU at the edge of some cornfield in the middle of nowhere, our support network consisting of near-strangers and people we had known for less than a year. I floored it. If nothing else I was determined to not have to deliver William myself in a Honda Civic on the side of a rural road.

It was all a mistake, I kept thinking to myself. The decision to move here, the decision to have a baby, everything that had happened since that first dumb story. I should have just left things as they were, moved on to other stories, continued living the D.C. life the way I had been. I'd be in the newsroom now, surrounded by colleagues, probably preparing for some TV or radio hit. Our lives would be smaller, circumscribed by the commute and the costs and everything that made us want to leave in the first place. But God damn it, at least we wouldn't be about to bring a strange new baby into the world six weeks prematurely in a frigid field in the ugliest county in America.

We made it to the hospital. I found a wheelchair and wheeled Briana in the main entrance. We had no idea where to go. There was a kindly old woman sitting at a volunteer station. We ran over there.

"Labor and delivery?" I asked.

"Well . . . let me see," she said, slowly rifling through a stack of papers on the table. "Hmm. Okay. All right. Now then. Could I get you to sign this pa—"

"WE'RE ABOUT TO HAVE A PREMATURE FUCKING BABY WHERE IS LABOR AND DELIV-ERY??"

Some of the staff overheard the outburst and quickly shuffled us off in the proper direction. They got us set up in a room and strapped the fetal heart rate monitor across Bri's belly. Two pieces of good news: we weren't going to deliver him in a field, and his heart rate was strong. Doctors and nurses came in, asked batteries of questions, checked monitors, and went out. Eventually several came in at once.

"Your baby is very early," a doctor said.

"Yes, we know."

"We don't have the facilities to handle a baby that pre-mature here," he said. "You'll have to go to Grand Forks."

Bri and I looked at each other.

"We have an ambulance ready with a team to accom-pany you," the doctor said. "If need be they'll be able to deliver the baby on the way."

"Only had to do that once so far, in seventeen years!" a chipper voice volunteered from the back of the crowd, the ambulance driver.

They loaded Bri on a stretcher with various machines and monitors in tow. They told me to follow in the car, and to not bother trying to keep up. "We'll be going fast and don't need any accidents," the driver said. Fine with me. I walked back to the car. I got in. I drove. As I crossed the bridge over the Red River of the North thirty minutes later, it struck me that we'd be having a North Dakota baby, not a Minnesota baby. It seemed so strange, and foreign. A child of the West, a frontier baby. To my knowledge no Ingraham had ever been born anywhere west of Niagara Falls. What the hell were we doing out here?

I got to the hospital in Grand Forks and found Briana in an upstairs delivery room. It was quiet and the lights were dim, almost peaceful. Back at Hopkins the twins had been born under harsh lights in an operating room with about two dozen people present, separate teams for each of the babies and one for mom in case things really went south. Here in North Dakota things were more laid-back, partly a simple function of there being only one baby. They gave Bri an epidural and kept an eye on her dilation. Jason texted asking if we needed anything. I sent him a list of things I had forgotten—my meds, a wallet, a phone charger.

About two hours after the contractions first started William was ready to be born. Like his brothers, he wasn't one to dilly-dally. A couple of doctors and nurses came in, Bri pushed once, and suddenly there he was: purple and wriggling, hollering his strange, raspy yowl. His vitals were good. His APGAR score was good. Miraculously, Bri got to hold him to her chest and sing to him for a few moments before they wheeled him away.

The NICU in Grand Forks was completely different

than the one in Johns Hopkins. The Hopkins NICU was home to rows upon rows of stalls, each of those home to a tiny person in an incubator. There were dozens of babies there. In my mind's eye it's vast. The memory of it reminds me of the scene in the *Matrix* where we see the massive facility housing the gel-filled holding cells where the robots harvest energy from twitching humans. The Grand Forks NICU was a single room, smaller than an elementary school class. There were one or two other babies in there but it was quiet. There was hardly any sound of alarms.

When we first went to see him, a few hours after his birth, William was sleeping peacefully on his back in a tight cozy swaddle, a blue and white cap keeping his head warm. His hair was dark like mine but he had a face like Briana's. He weighed a tad above five pounds, heavier than Charles had been but lighter than Jack. He arrived at almost the exact same gestational day of his pregnancy as his brothers had. Briana is nothing if not consistent.

I was rather snobbishly prepared to look down my nose at the NICU doctors—what deficiencies in their training had caused them to be out here in the sticks, in Grand Forks, rather than at a world-class facility like Hopkins? But of course this was stupid of me. The doctors were incredibly knowledgeable. When I offhandedly mentioned some protocol I had observed there that had been different than what they'd done at Hopkins with the twins, one of the doctors told me that new research had come out in the intervening years concluding that the protocol they were now using at Grand Forks was superior. This put me at ease: if these docs were up on the NICU research published since 2013 it was clear they knew what the hell they were doing.

More to the point, they were warmer toward us than the Hopkins doctors had been, almost more human. With just a few babies to manage they had time to talk to us, to answer our questions, to give us a clear sense of how William was doing and what we should expect in the days to come. He was a champ, as it turned out, mastering breathing within a few hours and getting a solid grasp on the breastfeeding stuff within days. The doctors kept warning us that he would probably crash, that NICU babies always do this, that after two or three days of progress something would go to hell and we'd be back at square one. Miraculously, it never happened. While the twins had spent six weeks at the hospital, William was on his way back to Red Lake Falls in less than five days. Our North Dakota baby was coming back east, coming home.

The temperatures warmed dramatically during those five days. There was still snow on the ground when we drove to the hospital in Crookston in a panic. Five days later it was 75 and sunny. The flowers were coming up. It was finally spring.

William's infancy was an odd paradox. On the one hand, it was infinitely easier to deal with just one baby at a time rather than two. On the other, having two toddlers to manage on top of the baby, with one of them on the autism spectrum, presented its own set of challenges.

But the greatest difference between William and the twins was time—time we simply hadn't had back in Baltimore. As an employee of the federal government Briana had a fairly generous paid-leave policy to draw on and she ended up taking about four months off following the birth of the twins, half paid, half unpaid. Four months is a lot, relative to the U.S. average. Nearly one-third of employed new moms don't take any maternity leave at all, according to federal statistics. The national average is just ten weeks. Among moms who do take time off, fully one-third are not paid for any portion of their time. The United States is the only country in the developed world, and one of the few in the entire world, that fails to mandate paid leave time for new moms.

Even though we knew we were fortunate, four months still felt like hardly enough time to spend with

Moving to greener places makes people happier

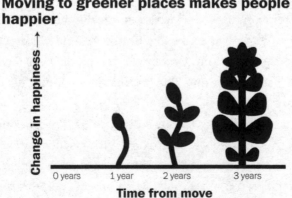

Source: Alcock et al., 2014

two tiny babies who had spent the first weeks of their life tethered to machines in an intensive care unit. But with William we didn't have to make that trade-off. Bri could be here, with him, giving him the direct parental care that he—and all babies—truly need. With William we've been able to experience and share his full childhood—the big milestones like walking and talking, of course, but thousands of little ones, too. His joy at seeing one of the cats jump off a table. His wonderment at a truck driving down the street. The touch of his tiny hand on one of our cheeks. The sweet smell of his round little head as he nuzzles into one of our shoulders to drift off to sleep. We felt, and still feel, incredibly fortunate to be able to have these everyday moments. We wish that we lived in a world where we didn't have to feel privileged to be able to have those moments together.

EPILOGUE

At the outset of our trip it wasn't clear how long it would all last. I had pitched my editors on a year, maybe two, who knows. Thankfully, they hadn't set any preconditions regarding my return. But the longer we've lived here, the more it seems clear that yes, we'll actually be staying here for good. Or at least for the foreseeable future.

As I write these words the twins are in kindergarten. I can hear Briana and William laughing outside, in the snow, from my office window. Every minute we're able to spend together here, as a family, is a reminder of the time we'd be forced to be apart if we were back in the city. With each passing day that old life becomes more unimaginable.

When people and places halfway across the country are just a mouse click away on your computer, it's easy to assume that we live in a nation made small and manageable by technology. But living in a place like Red Lake County, hours away from any major metro area, is a reminder that in much of the country, the rhythms of daily life are still markedly different than the coastal city grind of long commutes and high-octane jobs.

As somebody whose job is to write about "data" writ large, I'm a big believer in its power—better living through quantification. But my relocation to Red Lake Falls has been a humbling reminder of the limitations of numbers. It has opened my eyes to all the things that get lost when you abstract people, places, and points in time down to a single number on a computer screen.

The government's natural-amenities index captures the flatness of midwestern farm country quite well, for instance. But it misses out on so much about that landscape: the sound of the breeze rustling the grain or the way the wheat catches the light at different times of day, the dry-sweet smell of a field full of sunflowers.

Yes, that natural amenities index accurately captured the flatness. The summer heat. The bitter winter cold. But it doesn't tell you how a family can keep itself warm through the coldest of winters by building igloos and sledding down the town hill. Or how the vast winter night's sky shines with the light of thousands of stars that people who live in cities will never know. It doesn't tell you about the warmth put off by a big roaring fire in a town park at the darkest time of the year, how the light dances on the faces of the people gathered around.

Briana and I have lived together all over the country, including in New York, California, Vermont, and Maryland. But we've never lived in any place quite like this.

Most important, the data do not capture how moving to a place like this can be a life-altering experience for kids—for our twins, now six, who've now spent more birthdays in Minnesota than they did in Maryland. Or for little William, now two—a soul as dear to me as anyone I've ever known. There would have been no William had we stayed in Maryland. This whole new dimension of our lives, of familial love, would have remained shut off from us had we stayed there. Worse, we would never even have known what we were missing.

Here there is space for families to play, grow, expand. Space that doesn't exist where life is circumscribed by commutes and high costs and the presence of thousands, of millions of other people. If you keep a fish in a small crowded tank it will grow up stunted and tiny, never attaining its true natural size. Part of me believes that people are the same way, that we need space, room to explore and grow, a certain distance from our neighbors.

In that respect, at least, the Midwest has quite literally broadened our horizons.

One of the big dangers of our glorious, new, quantified world is the emergence of a type of numeric stereotyping—of insights hardened into dogma by the weight of a thousand datasets.

We "know," for instance, that Mississippi is poor, that New York City is expensive, that Chicago is violent, and that Red Lake County is ugly. These things are, of course, true in the aggregate sense, or in comparison with other places.

But each of these numbers and rankings masks infinite nuance behind their finite limits. They overlook the thriving communities in Mississippi, the inspiring stories of tenacity and triumph in Manhattan, and the people quietly working to make Chicago's streets safer.

And they can't, of course, capture the quiet peace of

A year in Red Lake Falls, by the numbers

Money saved on mortgage and childcare payments

$4,000
per month

Blood pressure decrease

30 *pts.*

Coldest temp. endured

-40
Fahrenheit

Hours of darkness on Dec. 21

16

Rabbits killed (accidentally)

Babies made

1

Times accused of stealing plums off neighbor's tree

1

an evening spent by the bluffs of the Red Lake River, watching your sons giggle as they toss sticks in the current while dragonflies dance overhead.

I've said it before and I'll say it one more time: it takes a place as small as Red Lake County to drive home just how big this country really is.

ACKNOWLEDGMENTS

This book would not have been possible without the contributions of the following people;

USDA economist David McGranahan, who in 1999 compiled the Natural Amenities Index, quietly planting the seeds of data that would upend my life sixteen years later;

Zach Goldfarb, who as my editor at the Washington Post in the summer of 2015 was surprisingly amenable to nearly every wild story idea I threw at him;

The anonymous individuals behind the Indignant Minnesotan Twitter account, who fanned the initial flames of polite outrage in response to my original story on Red Lake County;

Every indignant Minnesotan who wrote to me in defense of the beauty of their state in the summer of 2015, of whom there are far too many to mention individually;

Every indifferent North Dakotan who did not write to me in the summer of 2015 despite their state's poor showing on the Natural Amenities Index, which served as a tacit confirmation that Minnesota really is someplace special;

Jason Brumwell, whose cordial invitation convinced me to actually visit the place I had trash-talked in the pages of a national newspaper, and who's done so much since then to make me feel at home here;

Dick Brumwell, who's worked so hard to ensure I experience everything Minnesota has to offer, from corn shocks to ice fishing;

The rest of the Brumwell clan, including Ryan, Kristin, Steph, Joe, Heather, and Wade, who have truly become our Minnesota family;

My mom, whose spirit of adventure spurred us to move here to begin with;

My dad, who inspired me to become a writer;

My agent, Rafe Sagalyn, who shepherded this book from idea to proposal to first draft;

My editor, Sara Nelson, who shaped my messy manuscript into a coherent narrative;

The publishing team at HarperCollins, including Jane Beirn, who's done so much to get the word out; Mary Gaule, who's patiently guided me through the publishing process; Hannah Bishop, for her invaluable logistical work; and Christine Choe for her social media expertise;

Editors and managers at the Washington Post, who were shockingly receptive when I pitched them on moving out of D. C. and into the middle of nowhere;

Missy and Danny Maurstad, who showed us the true meaning of Minnesota kindness;

Jim Benoit, for his always-entertaining bullshitting;

Larry Eukel, for welcoming us to the neighborhood and rescuing our idiot cat that one time;

Acknowledgments

John and Sandy Klein, for helping make our dream of a Minnesota home a reality;

Rob and Alice Conwell, for introducing us to the northwest Minnesota arts scene;

Jack, Charles, and William, who inspired Briana and me to seek a better life to begin with;

And Briana, for being my steadfast partner throughout this long, ridiculous, beautiful adventure.

BIBLIOGRAPHY

Prologue

Berry, Brian J. L., and Adam Okulicz-Kozaryn. "An Urban-Rural Happiness Gradient." *Urban Geography* 32, no. 6 (2011): 871–83.

Pew Research Center. "Political Polarization in the American Public." June 2014. Accessed March 4, 2019. https://www.pewresearch.org /wp-content/uploads/sites/4/2014/06/6-12-2014-Political-Polarization -Release.pdf.

United States Census Bureau. "New Census Data Show Differences Between Urban and Rural Populations." December 8, 2016. Accessed March 4, 2019. https://www.census.gov/newsroom/press -releases/2016/cb16-210.html.

———. "QuickFacts: Red Lake County, Minnesota." Accessed March 4, 2019. https://www.census.gov/quickfacts/redlakecounty minnesota.

United States Department of Agriculture. "Natural Amenities Scale." Last modified February 26, 2018. https://www.ers.usda.gov /data-products/natural-amenities-scale/.

Chapter 1

Cook, Philip J. *Paying the Tab*. Princeton, NJ: Princeton University Press, 2007.

Ferguson, Todd W. and Jeffrey A. Tamburello. "The Natural Environment as a Spiritual Resource: A Theory of Regional Variation in Religious Adherence." *Sociology of Religion* 76, no. 3 (2015): 295–324.

Glaeser, Edward L., Joshua D. Gottlieb, and Oren Ziv. "Unhappy Cities." National Bureau of Economic Research, 2014. https://www .nber.org/papers/w20291.

Glaeser, Edward L., and Kristina Tobio. "The Rise of the Sunbelt." Taubman Center Policy Brief, May 2007. https://www.hks .harvard.edu/sites/default/files/centers/taubman/files/sunbelt .pdf.

Helliwell, John F., Hugh Shiplett, and Christopher P. Barrington-Leigh. "How Happy Are Your Neighbours? Variation in Life Satisfaction among 1200 Canadian Neighbourhoods and Communities." National Bureau of Economic Research, May 2018. https://www.nber.org/papers/w24592.

Kanazawa, S., and N. P. Li. "Country Roads, Take Me Home . . . To My Friends: How Intelligence, Population Density, and Friendship Affect Modern Happiness." *British Journal of Psychology* 107, no. 4 (2016): 675–97.

Kwon, Diana. "Does City Life Pose a Risk to Mental Health?" *Scientific American,* May 20, 2016. https://www.scientificamerican.com/article/does-city-life-pose-a-risk-to-mental-health/.

McKinney, Matt. "Minnesotans Seeing Red over Washington Post List of Desirable Counties to Live In." *Minneapolis Star-Tribune,* August 20, 2015. http://www.startribune.com/washington-post-reporter-says-minnesota-is-ugly-minnesotans-politely-beg-to-differ/322350791/.

Rietmulder, Michael. "Minnesota's Red Lake County Named America's Worst Place to Live." *City Pages,* August 19, 2015. http://www.citypages.com/news/minnesotas-red-lake-county-named-americas-worst-place-to-live-7577959.

United States Census Bureau. "American Community Survey." Accessed March 4, 2019. https://www.census.gov/programs-surveys/acs.

———. "QuickFacts: Oneonta City, New York." Accessed March 4, 2019. https://www.census.gov/quickfacts/fact/table/oneontacitynewyork/PST045217.

United States Department of Agriculture. "Census of Agriculture." Accessed March 4, 2019. https://www.nass.usda.gov/AgCensus/.

Chapter 2

Graf, Nikki. "Most Americans Say Children Are Better Off with a Parent at Home." Pew Research Center, October 10, 2016. http://www.pewresearch.org/fact-tank/2016/10/10/most-americans-say-children-are-better-off-with-a-parent-at-home/.

Ihrke, David. "Reason for Moving: 2012 to 2013." United States Census Bureau, Last modified June 2014. https://www.census.gov/prod/2014pubs/p20-574.pdf.

Lucas-Thompson, Rachel G., Wendy A. Goldberg, and JoAnn Prause. "Maternal Work Early in the Lives of Children and Its Distal Associations with Achievement and Behavior Problems: A Meta-Analysis." *Psychological Bulletin* 136, no. 6 (2010): 915–42.

Chapter 3

Ford, Carmel. "Number of Bathrooms in New Homes." NAHB Eye on Housing, December 7, 2017. http://eyeonhousing.org/2017/12/number-of-bathrooms-in-new-homes/.

Ingraham, Christopher. "Lawns Are a Soul-Crushing Timesuck and Most of Us Would Be Better Off Without Them." *Washington Post*, August 4, 2015. https://www.washingtonpost.com/news/wonk/wp/2015/08/04/lawns-are-a-soul-crushing-timesuck-and-most-of-us-would-be-better-off-without-them.

United States Department of Health and Human Services. "Adolescents and Tobacco: Trends." Last modified September 23, 2016. https://www.hhs.gov/ash/oah/adolescent-development/substance-use/drugs/tobacco/trends/index.html.

Chapter 5

Harvard University. "Project Implicit." Accessed March 4, 2019. https://implicit.harvard.edu/implicit/takeatest.html.

ICPSR. "Uniform Crime Reporting Program Data: County-Level Detailed Arrest and Offense Data, United States, 2014." September 12, 2017. https://www.icpsr.umich.edu/icpsrweb/ICPSR/studies/36399.

Ingraham, Christopher. "It's Not Just Rand Paul's Street: Americans Are a Lot Less Neighborly than They Used to Be." *Washington Post*, November 7, 2017. https://www.washingtonpost.com/news/wonk/wp/2017/11/07/its-not-just-rand-pauls-street-americans-are-a-lot-less-neighborly-than-they-used-to-be.

———. "The Most Racist Places in America, According to Google." *Washington Post*, April 28, 2015. https://www.washingtonpost.com/news/wonk/wp/2015/04/28/the-most-racist-places-in-america-according-to-google/.

Moore, Peter. "Obama Isn't the Only One Who Doesn't Lock the Door." YouGov, September 30, 2014. https://today.yougov.com/topics/lifestyle/articles-reports/2014/09/30/obama-isnt-only-one-who-doesnt-lock-doors.

Opportunity Insights. "The Opportunity Atlas." Accessed March 4, 2019. https://www.opportunityatlas.org/.

Chapter 6

Belluz, Julia. "The Historically Low Birthrate, Explained in 3 Charts." Vox.com, May 22, 2018. https://www.vox.com/science-and-health/2018/5/22/17376536/fertility-rate-united-states-births-women.

Ingraham, Christopher. "The Absolute Best Place to Grow Up in America." *Washington Post*, June 24, 2016. https://www.washington

post.com/news/wonk/wp/2016/06/24/the-absolute-best-place-to
-grow-up-in-america.

———. "Start Saving Now: Day Care Costs More than College in 31 States." *Washington Post*, April 9, 2014. https://www.washington post.com/news/wonk/wp/2014/04/09/start-saving-now-day-care -costs-more-than-college-in-31-states/.

Lam, Onyi, Brian Broderick, and Skye Toor. "How Far Americans Live from the Closest Hospital Differs by Community Type." Pew Research Center, December 12, 2018. http://www.pewresearch.org /fact-tank/2018/12/12/how-far-americans-live-from-the-closest -hospital-differs-by-community-type/.

Mackin, Amy. "How My Autistic Son Got Lost in the Public School System." *Atlantic*, January 3, 2013. https://www.theatlantic.com /national/archive/2013/01/how-my-autistic-son-got-lost-in-the -public-school-system/266782/.

National Trust. "Jock VI of Chartwell." Accessed March 4, 2019. https://www.nationaltrust.org.uk/chartwell/features/jock-vi-of -chartwell.

Stone, Lyman. "American Women Are Having Fewer Children than They'd Like." *New York Times*, February 13, 2018. https://www .nytimes.com/2018/02/13/upshot/american-fertility-is-falling -short-of-what-women-want.html.

Chapter 7

Harveson, Robert M. "History of Sugarbeets." Accessed March 4, 2019. https://cropwatch.unl.edu/history-sugarbeets.

Kilgannon, Corey. "For Hunters in the Woods, a Quiet Killer: Tree Stands." *New York Times*, December 22, 2017. https://www.nytimes .com/2017/12/22/nyregion/for-hunters-in-the-woods-a-quiet-killer -tree-stands.html.

Li, Yong-Xiang, Torbjorn Tornqvist, Johanna M. Nevitt, and Barry Kohl. "Synchronizing a Sea-Level Jump, Final Lake Agassiz Drainage, and Abrupt Cooling 8200 Years Ago." *Earth and Planetary Science Letters* 315–16 (2012): 41–50.

United States Department of Agriculture. "U.S. Sugar Production." Accessed March 4, 2019. https://www.ers.usda.gov/topics/crops /sugar-sweeteners/background/.

United States Fish & Wildlife Service. "National Survey— Overview." Last modified May 2, 2018. https://wsfrprograms.fws .gov/subpages/nationalsurvey/national_survey.htm.

Chapter 8

Bloch, Matthew, Larry Buchanan, Josh Katz, and Kevin Quealy. "An Extremely Detailed Map of the 2016 Election." *New York Times*, July 25, 2018. https://www.nytimes.com/interactive/2018 /upshot/election-2016-voting-precinct-maps.html#8.22/39.225 /-78.231.

Bump, Philip. "Donald Trump Will Be President Thanks to 80,000 People in Three States." *Washington Post*. December 1, 2016. https://www.washingtonpost.com/news/the-fix/wp/2016/12/01 /donald-trump-will-be-president-thanks-to-80000-people-in -three-states/.

Centers for Disease Control and Prevention. "Firearm Mortality by State." Accessed March 4, 2019. https://www.cdc.gov/nchs/press room/sosmap/firearm_mortality/firearm.htm.

Kalesan, B., M. D. Villarreal, K. M. Keyes, et al. "Gun Owner- ship and Social Gun Culture." *Injury Prevention* 22, no. 3 (2016): 216–20.

McCourt School of Public Policy. "The Lugar Center, McCourt Unveil 2017 Bipartisan Index." Accessed March 4, 2019. https:// mccourt.georgetown.edu/bipartisan-index.

Minnesota Secretary of State. "Election Results." Accessed March 4, 2019. https://www.sos.state.mn.us/elections-voting/election-results/.

Winchester, Ben. "A Rural Brain Gain Migration." University of Minnesota Extension. Accessed March 4, 2019. https://extension .umn.edu/economic-development/rural-brain-gain-migration.

Chapter 9

Pete Boulay. "The Mysterious July 4th Snows of Minnesota." Minnesota Climatology Working Group. Accessed March 4, 2019. http://climateapps.dnr.state.mn.us/doc/journal/july_snow .htm.

National Oceanic and Atmospheric Administration. "National Snow Analyses." Accessed March 4, 2019. https://www.nohrsc.noaa .gov/nsa/.

Rao, Maya. "For Snowmobilers, 2014 Was a Deadly Year." *Minne- apolis Star-Tribune*, January 6, 2015. http://www.startribune.com /for-snowmobilers-2014-was-a-deadly-year/287426421/.

Tweet by @mberkowski, December 28, 2018, https://twitter.com /mberkowski/status/1078632108208386048.

Chapter 10

Health Resources and Services Administration. "Maternity Leave." Accessed March 4, 2019. https://mchb.hrsa.gov/whusa11 /hstat/hsrmh/downloads/pdf/233ml.pdf.

Misra, Joya. "The US Is Stingier with Child Care and Maternity Leave than the Rest of the World." The Conversation, April 19, 2018. https://theconversation.com/the-us-is-stingier-with-child-care -and-maternity-leave-than-the-rest-of-the-world-94770.

ABOUT THE AUTHOR

CHRISTOPHER INGRAHAM writes about all things data, with a particular interest in wealth, income, and inequality. He previously worked at the Brookings Institution and the Pew Research Center.